Journeys
through
Dreamtime

Journeys
through
Dreamtime

OCEANIAN MYTH

MYTH AND MANKIND

JOURNEYS THROUGH DREAMTIME: Oceanian Myth
Writers: Tony Allan (An Unseen World, The Oceanian Legacy)
Fergus Fleming (The Myriad Beliefs of Melanesia, Polynesian Paradise)
Michael Kerrigan (A Timeless Land, The Rich Cycle of Life)
Consultant: Dr Chris Gosden

Created, edited and designed by
Duncan Baird Publishers
Castle House
75–76 Wells Street
London W1P 3RE

DUNCAN BAIRD PUBLISHERS
Managing Editor: Diana Loxley
Managing Art Editor: Gabriella Le Grazie
Series Editor: Christopher Westhorp
Editor: Christopher Westhorp
Designer: Christine Keilty
Picture Researchers: Anne-Marie Ehrlich, Susannah Stone
and Cecilia Weston-Baker
Commissioned Illustrations: Neil Gower
Map Artwork: Lorraine Harrison
Artwork Borders: Iona McGlashan
Editorial Researcher: Clare Richards
Editorial Assistant: Lucy Rix

TIME-LIFE BOOKS
Time-Life INC. President and CEO: George Artandi
Time-Life International President: Stephen R. Frary

Staff for JOURNEYS THROUGH DREAMTIME: Oceanian Myth
Editorial Manager: Tony Allan
Design Consultant: Mary Staples
Editorial Production: Ruth Vos

Published by Time-Life Books BV, Amsterdam
First Time-Life English language printing 1999
TIME-LIFE is a trademark of
Time Warner Inc, USA

ISBN 0 7054 3623 3

Colour separation by Colourscan, Singapore
Printed and bound by Milanostampa, SpA, Farigliano, Italy

Title page: **An Arnhem Land bark painting by Aboriginal artist Munyal depicts the use of a trap made from the pandanus shrub, one of many different methods of catching fish.**

Contents page: **A Chambri Lakes food hook or** *ishambwan,* **New Guinea. The design represents a celebration of a totemic ancestor.**

30 29 28 27 26 25 24 23 22 21 20 19 18 17 16 15 14 13 12 11 10 9 8 7 6 5 4 3

Contents

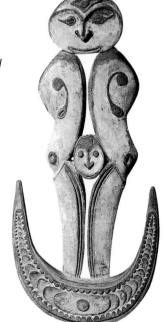

AN UNSEEN WORLD

For the Aborigines of Australia, there were always two kinds of reality. One was the everyday life of the world around them. The other, just as alive and compelling, was the *Altjeringa* or "Dreamtime". This was the age at the world's dawn when a giant ancestor race had walked the land, moulding its contours and stocking it with its familiar freight of plants and animals. And where they went they left traces of themselves that made certain spots sacred. These numinous areas, together with the magical songs and objects that the ancestral beings bequeathed to their human successors, formed the heart of the Aborigines' spiritual heritage.

For "the dreaming" was never simply a thing of the past. Not just in Australia itself but in all the many islands that make up Oceania, the stories handed down from generation to generation were an essential part of day-to-day existence. Each mountain and glade, every waterhole and atoll, had a spirit presence. These silent guardians could be benign or malevolent, but always required respectful treatment. If due observance of custom was neglected, their anger could be terrible.

Australasia's two main components have had very different histories. The continent of Australia itself has one of the most ancient populations on Earth; the Aborigine peoples have inhabited it continuously for maybe as much as 65,000 years. In contrast, many of the Oceanian islands were settled relatively recently; New Zealand, for example, has seen barely 1,000 years of human habitation.

Yet for all their differences, the peoples who occupy this vast and scattered region share much in common from the point of view of myth. One idea that is widespread is the concept of a spiritual power that can exist in people or in places, in actions as well as objects, and whoever or whatever possesses it must be respected and feared.

The notion is at its purest in Polynesia, where it is called *mana*, but under different names it resonates across the entire region. For all the area's indigenous peoples have traditionally lived in a world in which unseen forces are constantly shaping people's destinies. To comprehend them they turn to myth, looking to the traditional tales passed down by their ancestors to map out their daily conduct and to explain the mysterious and often unpredictable workings of fate.

Opposite: **Dramatic rock art is found throughout the Australian landscape. This ancient x-ray painting of spirit figures and heroes is at Nourlangie Rock, Alligator River, in eastern Arnhem Land.**

Below: **A wooden, painted mask from New Ireland, used in ceremonial feasts to honour the ancestors. Such masks were highly individual in design and localized in meaning.**

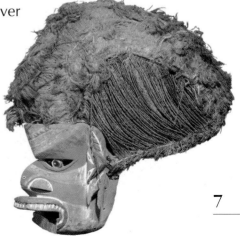

The First Australasians

Even more than in other parts of the world, the physical backdrop has shaped Australasia's myths. One major factor has been the Pacific Ocean, the world's largest ocean, which in its entirety covers one-third of the globe.

Scattered across it are more than 20,000 islands that together make up a land area of 1,300,000 square kilometres, a deceptively high figure as nine-tenths of it is accounted for by New Guinea and New Zealand. The others range from medium-sized bodies a few hundred square kilometres across to tiny, uninhabited pimples. Their isolation amid the ocean's vastness has led to a fragmentation of belief, with each different community telling its own version of the primal legends.

The sheer vastness of the region's other component, the continent-sized island of Australia, similarly served to segregate its peoples and diversify their myths. At 7,682,300 square kilometres, its land area is half as big again as Europe to the Russian border. Roughly two-thirds is taken up by the Outback, a parched plateau that supports a sparse and diffuse population. Although continent-wide connections existed, the bush's distances cut settlers off from one another much as the Pacific's did, ensuring that Aboriginal oral traditions are almost as varied as the Oceanian islanders'.

The Settling of Sahul

Although the environment may never have been exactly welcoming, the configuration of the continent was very different when the first settlers

arrived. At that time Australia, Tasmania and New Guinea were joined in a single landmass, known to geologists as Sahul. The world was experiencing an Ice Age, and sea levels had fallen to perhaps 100 metres below their present level.

The first colonists came to Sahul from the Indonesian islands to the north. They could well have travelled all the way from the Asian mainland without ever having to travel more than 100 kilometres over open sea; the final hop, from Timor to the Kimberley Plateau, would have been the longest: a journey of just eighty-seven kilometres. Furthermore, those who made it could well have known there was land waiting at the end, for the smoke from naturally occurring bush fires – still a common occurrence – can be seen in optimal conditions as much as 110 kilometres away.

Nobody knows exactly when the first humans arrived in Sahul, though in recent years the date has been pushed steadily further back into prehistory. Until recently, the oldest known remains were of campsites that radio-carbon dating showed to have been inhabited 35,000 to 40,000 years ago. In the 1990s, a skeleton at Kow Swamp was identified as being over 60,000 years old. The site lies in northern Victoria, a long way from any point of arrival on the continent, so if the much-disputed dating is confirmed, it suggests an initial landfall more than 60,000 years ago. Less contentious, however, are Northern Territory finds which date a human presence to 65,000 years ago.

No remnants of early boats have survived, but the assumption is that the newcomers drifted across the straits from Indonesia on rafts made of lashed strips of bamboo or mangrove wood. They would have found a land quite unlike the one they had left behind, for the southern continent's long isolation had given it a unique fauna of marsupials in place of the placental mammals familiar everywhere else in the world. Yet for all its strangeness, the environment was not unwelcoming. There was plentiful game, few carnivorous animals to compete for it and no hostile tribes.

The land itself, though hardly fertile, was at least less prone to natural disasters than the seismically active regions through which the immigrants must have travelled. The major volcanic activity that had shaped Sahul's mountains had ceased some 100 million years before. Except in the east where there were more recent peaks, the first Australians found a stable landscape of seemingly endless plains and low, eroded hills, along with huge lakes that periodically dried up and a vegetation dominated by eucalyptuses and acacias.

The people who made the crossing were almost certainly Australoids, members of a group distinguished by dark skin and a flat, retreating forehead whose surviving representatives include the Aborigines and the inhabitants of many Melanesian islands today. Some scholars have argued that their predecessors on the Asian mainland may even have traced their ancestry all the

The vast Outback is an overwhelmingly flat and parched landscape. When rock formations, such as the Devil's Marbles near Alice Springs, do occur they appear strangely out of place and are visible from miles around in every direction.

way back to *Homo erectus*, a predecessor of *Homo sapiens* known to have been living in China as much as 200,000 years ago.

Once they had reached the new continent the incomers spread out across its vast expanses, following the river systems inland. They moved north into what was to become New Guinea, where stone axes and a flaked blade found on the Huon peninsula have been dated back to 40,000BC. Some 10,000 years later – perhaps much earlier – they were in present-day New South Wales, where the now-dry bed of Lake Mungo has preserved one of Australia's best studied sites. In it was found the skeleton of a tall man carefully buried in a shallow grave, with traces of powdered ochre sprinkled over him. Even more intriguing were the remains of a woman who had been laid to rest at the same site 5,000 years afterwards. Her corpse was cremated and the bones were smashed to pieces before being interred in a pit. Aborigines in eastern Australia are known to have buried their dead this way as recently as the nineteenth century.

By 35,000BC the settlers seem to have reached the continent's farthest corners. Even Tasmania had been peopled by then, making its inhabitants probably the Earth's southernmost people during the last Ice Age. They were still there 26,000 years later, when a period of global warming raised sea levels enough both to cut off Tasmania from the mainland and to separate Australia from New Guinea. After more than ten millennia of isolation, cut off from their neighbours by the Bass Strait, the Tasmanians finally found a force they could not

survive: within 100 years of white men settling the island the population had been almost wiped out by rifles, disease and demoralization, and in 1876 the last full-blooded Tasmanian died. (Mixed-blood descendants keep the culture alive today.)

Australian Tribal Life

Elsewhere across the continent, the Aborigines fanned out in small hunter-gathering bands, typically ranging in size from fifty up to 500 people all claiming a common ancestry. Each would have its own estate, a patch of territory over which it claimed pre-eminent rights. Occasionally, tribes would join up with their neighbours – often more distant kinsmen – to forage over a wider area or to participate in gatherings known as corroborees. These were principally social occasions enlivened by music-making and dances, though they also provided an opportunity for trading and the passing on of myths and legends.

Through these informal contacts a system of trade and cultural routes eventually came to span the continent. Shells from the far north found their way to the south coast 3,000 kilometres away, bartered from tribe to tribe. Stories too passed down the line. Although there was never any such thing as a pan-Aboriginal mythology, individual tales, of a great flood or of the Rainbow Snake that helped to shape the landscape, were transmitted orally at campfire gatherings until they had spread across most parts of the country.

Within the tribes life was egalitarian; social and economic hierarchies were mostly notable by their absence. Individuals acquired influence through force of personality, hunting prowess or exceptional knowledge of mythical lore rather than through birth or background. Yet kinship was

A didjeridoo collected from Arnhem Land's Yirrkala people this century. The design is in sacred ochre and refers to Bodngu, the Thunder Man. The stripes refer to *larrpan,* or thunderbolts, and the broken lines to water or rain.

The fireside corroboree provided the social setting for music and dancing, as well as the opportunity to transmit long, often complex myths, sometimes in the form of song-cycles. Painted by Samuel Thomas Gill in 1874.

centrally important, not merely in binding communities and clans together but also in forging links with the natural world. Stories of the Dreamtime told how remote ancestors at the dawn of time had created not just people but also birds, beasts and the natural world, forming ties that continued ever after to bond individuals with their surroundings.

The Dreamtime tales were at the heart of Aboriginal mythology. They told of an age long before human beings had made their appearance when the landscape was still malleable, waiting to be moulded. Some of the stories of giant creator beings may have been influenced by discoveries of the bones of extinct beasts, while tales of a great flood may have preserved folk memories of the time at the end of the Ice Age when sea levels rose dramatically and some regions were submerged.

The Outback environment also impinged on the myths in less direct ways. The scarcity of rainfall made the weather a central focus of concern, and spirits of lightning, thunder and rain all played a major role. Sometimes the aridity of the land was explained by reference to the excessive appetites of Sky Heroes, gigantic beings from primeval times whose great thirst drained the rivers and lakes and whose insatiable hunger decimated the continent's game. Naturally enough there were marked variations in the tales handed down by coastal and inland peoples, with the coast-dwellers telling of cultural heroes who arrived from across the waters whereas the Aborigines of the interior spoke of equivalent beings rising from the ground or descending from the sky. The lie of the land also lay behind the conservative and introspective character of the stories, which reflected the realities of a continent that was both geologically stable and relatively unaffected by outside influences until the recent coming of Europeans.

Native New Guinea

As Australia's companion in Sahul, New Guinea shared much of its early prehistory and was originally settled by people of the same Australoid stock. Climate-warming later broke the land-bridge with Australia and turned New Guinea into a separate island.

The most widely accepted theory holds that the first inhabitants reached New Guinea on foot from a landfall on what was later to be the Australian coast, but the possibility remains that they arrived by boat from the Indonesian islands.

The early hunter-gatherer colonizers took some time to penetrate the island's interior, though evidence from the Eastern Highlands indicates that it was inhabited by about 25,000BC. The first signs of forest clearance, indicating that cultivation might have begun, predate the climatic warming that broke the land-bridge and turned New Guinea into an island.

Excavations at Kuk in the centre of the island have revealed traces of drainage ditches which date to 7000BC, probably used in the cultivation of taro, a regional staple grown for its edible roots. Several millennia later pigs and dogs made a first appearance on the island.

These innovations, together with the discovery of some pottery and tools of polished stone, argue for the arrival of a fresh wave of immigrants who were culturally distinct from the Australoids. Linguists have dubbed them the Austronesians, early speakers of a language whose family now has some 800 branches, not only in Oceania but in Malaysia, Indonesia, the Philippines, Taiwan, Vietnam, Cambodia and even Madagascar. The range indicates the extent of the Austronesian peoples' travels and has led scholars to suggest that their original homeland was in southeast Asia, possibly in Taiwan.

The Oceania region is vast, embracing millions of square kilometres of ocean, a large continent and tens of thousands of islands and atolls whose inhabitants' distinctive cultures are grouped as Australian, Polynesian, Micronesian and Melanesian.

The Austronesians added ethnic variety to a geographically complex land whose communities were cut off from one another by its length of almost 2,500 kilometres, a ridge of high peaks running down the island's spine, swamps and impenetrable jungle, all of which made communication very difficult except by river.

The result in terms of myth and belief systems has been a quite exceptional diversity. New Guinea's peoples are isolated in pockets of habitation that not only often have different customs to their neighbours but frequently speak a separate language. More than 700 tongues have been identified – about one-seventh of the world's total.

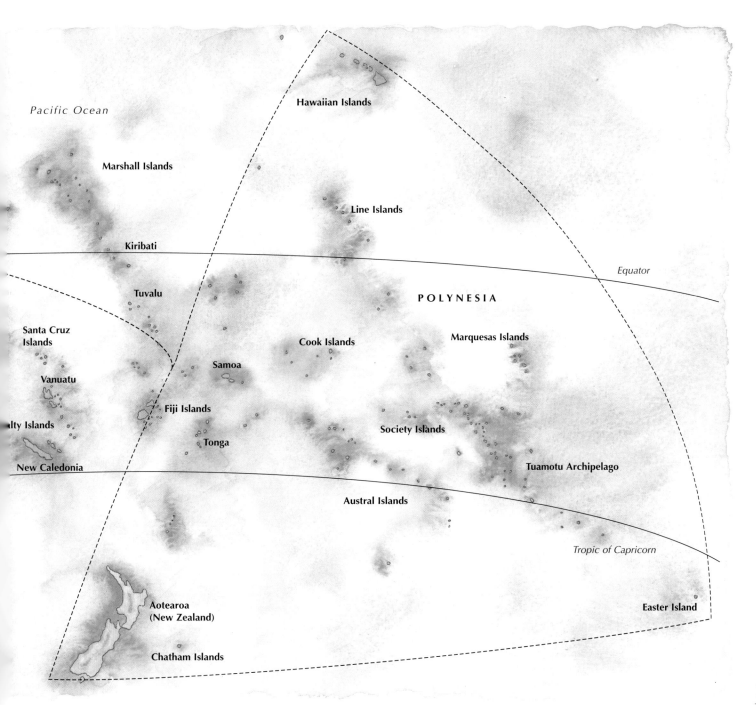

Pacific Ocean

Hawaiian Islands

Marshall Islands

Line Islands

Kiribati

Equator

Tuvalu

POLYNESIA

Santa Cruz Islands

Cook Islands

Marquesas Islands

Samoa

Vanuatu

Fiji Islands

lty Islands

Society Islands

Tonga

New Caledonia

Tuamotu Archipelago

Austral Islands

Tropic of Capricorn

Aotearoa (New Zealand)

Easter Island

Chatham Islands

The Melanesian Melting Pot

The islands of Melanesia spread north and eastwards of New Guinea, and the first to be inhabited were settled when New Guinea still formed part of Sahul. The earliest signs of human presence yet found were on New Ireland in the Bismarck Archipelago, where a cave at Matenkupkum was used as a shelter about 33,000 years ago. A 29,000-year-old site has also been found on the island of Buka, northernmost of the adjoining Solomon Islands.

The first arrivals must have been Australoid cousins of the original settlers of Australia and New Guinea. They spread out around the islands of western Melanesia, establishing trading networks as they went. The hard glass known as obsidian, obtained from a source on New Britain, has been found at early sites on other islands in the Bismarck Archipelago, indicating that it was being transported by boat at least by 15,000BC and possibly much earlier.

On present evidence, though, the original settlers were not long-distance sailors, and confined their voyages to island-hopping. The opening of eastern Melanesia had to wait for the arrival of the Austronesians sometime around 3500BC. They carried with them their usual cultural baggage of taro and yam cultivation, pigs, dogs and chickens. They also brought a new knowledge of ocean travel, for they may well have been the world's first true long-distance seafarers.

The vessels may have been dug-out canoes, the stability of which they increased by adding balancing outriggers, kept to windward when at sea. This made longer voyages possible, and was to play a crucial part in opening up not only Melanesia but all the Pacific islands to settlement.

Spear-wielding Solomon Island warriors greet the arrival of a canoe-borne party, c. 1930, perhaps fellow tribesmen returning from a headhunting and slave-taking expedition. The canoes had towering prows and were decorated with geometric patterns and designs of both spirit figures and fish.

Lapita Culture

As it happens, one important group of Austronesian-speakers left clear archaeological evidence of their progress in the form of a distinctive type of pottery. Lapita ware, so-called from the name of the site in New Caledonia where it was discovered in 1950, was a form of earthenware tempered with sand and fired over open flames. Often plain, it was otherwise decoratively patterned with the aid of a toothed implement similar to one still used in Polynesia for tattooing.

The earliest Lapita pottery yet found dates from about 1300BC and comes from the Bismarck Archipelago. From there the trail leads eastwards, mapping the progress of its makers as they made their way from island to island. All the early sites are coastal, confirming the impression that the Lapita people were mariners, though they relied on crops as well as fish for their sustenance. To judge from the evidence of the pottery, they were the first people to colonize the islands of eastern Melanesia beyond the Solomons, reaching Fiji – Melanesia's farthest outpost – in about 1100BC. They did not stop there, travelling on into Polynesia as far as Tonga and Samoa. There the trail ends, though the pottery continued to be made on existing sites for many centuries to come.

A figurehead or *kesoko* from the Solomon Islands that would have been positioned on the canoe prow. Made of wood and pearl shell inlay, it was used to ward off water spirits.

A Diversity of Societies

Melanesia's lengthy history of human occupation – the longest of any of the Pacific island groups – combined with the ethnic mix to create an extremely heterogeneous society. The linguistic divisions have continued to this day, with the Papuan languages of the original Australoid inhabitants being spoken in most of New Guinea and in parts of the Bismarck Archipelago and Solomon Islands chains, while Austronesian tongues predominate elsewhere.

Although there was always great variety among the various islands, social structures tended on the whole to be local and on a small scale. The focal point was usually the village or group of villages rather than the tribe or any other larger political grouping. The tenor of life was egalitarian; only Fiji and New Caledonia, where Polynesian influences were strong, had a complex social hierarchy and dominant hereditary chiefs.

Instead, power usually devolved locally onto "big men", who won the support of their neighbours through force of personality and by giving feasts and gifts. The headmen were usually expected to consult with village elders, who sat in council to deliver judgement on such matters as disputed land ownership or accusations of theft or witchcraft.

The centre of power in many villages was the men's house, where women and children were not admitted. These all-male sanctuaries often had religious importance for the whole community; tribal myths were recounted to initiates and sacred objects such as masks and carvings were also kept there. Some of these accoutrements had sound-producing qualities, ranging from the reedy notes of bamboo flutes to the growl of bullroarers; the men would use deception to buttress their position by telling the women and children that the strange noises they produced were the voices of spirits.

A Localized Mythology

Melanesian myths reflected the diversity and the local emphasis of the societies that produced them. There were few creation stories explaining the origin of the universe or the human race as a whole. These were normally taken as given, and the tales concentrated instead on the shaping of the landscape or the establishment of the existing social order.

Similarly, the Melanesians had no recurring hierarchies of gods. Rather, the most common mythical beings were culture heroes or ancestral spirits, the two often being one and the same. The tales were firmly rooted in the immediate neighbourhood of the people who told them, with all significant physical features of the landscape having their own spirit occupants. Everywhere there was a belief in a life after death; typically, the souls of the dead were considered to have journeyed to some specified mountain or a distant island.

Mapping Micronesia

Many of these features recurred in the myths of Micronesia, the island group to Melanesia's north. Although its constituent parts shared many cultural features with Melanesia, their physical conformation was often very different, for they are formed of basalt rocks extruded from ancient, long-inert volcanoes. Some of the islands, notably in the Marianas and Caroline groups, have kept their old volcanic form and rise dramatically from the

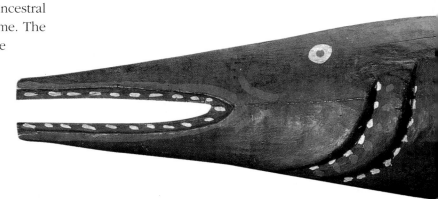

The Oceanian Tool Kit

Metals were unknown throughout Australasia, but the settlers showed great skill and ingenuity in fashioning utensils from the materials that were to hand.

On the Australian mainland, scrapers and clay heating bricks have been found in archaeological sites dating back 30,000 years. In later times men typically carried wooden spears, and the spearthrowers known as *woomeras*, while women had digging sticks and sometimes baskets of bark or plaited leaves for carrying food. Boomerangs were kept mainly for sport or ceremonial use, though hunters sometimes threw them to scare animals into traps.

Fishing was vitally important for the Oceanian islanders as well as for Australia's coastal peoples, and much care went into the preparation of fish-hooks, nets and traps. The hooks were usually made of shell, which also served to make knives, scrapers and bodily decorations. Stone served for axes, adzes and clubs, as well as occasionally for monumental building, while wood – often beautifully carved – was used to make gardening implements, paddles and axe-handles. Curiously the art of pottery-making, which was once common throughout the area, died out in Polynesia early in the first millennium AD; no satisfactory reason for its disappearance has yet emerged.

A decorated Maori cutting tool with an edge created from inset shark's teeth.

ocean, but many others are low-lying coral atolls. Indeed, eastern Micronesia's Marshall and Kiribati groups could be said to be the coral island's pre-eminent home.

Micronesia's past has been less thoroughly mapped than that of either Melanesia or Polynesia, but the evidence suggests that it was peopled by two different groups of Austronesians, one approaching from the east and the other from the west. Apparently neither belonged to the

Vanuatu, suggesting that incomers from those regions were the original colonizers. Yet social organization in these islands had more in common with Polynesia to the east, with hereditary rulers and social hierarchies playing a more prominent role than in Melanesia. One such dynasty created the region's best-known archaeological site, at Nan Madol on Pohnpei island in the Carolines, where the ruins of an ancient ceremonial centre stand on artificial islets in a shallow lagoon.

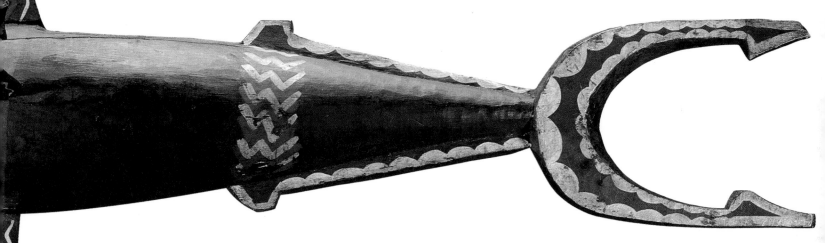

Lapita culture, as none of the pottery has yet been discovered there.

Linguistic evidence, backed by findings of non-Lapita pottery, indicate that the Marianas and Palau to the west were colonized from what are now the Philippines. These islands were probably the first in Micronesia to be inhabited; certainly the earliest-known sites, dating back to approximately 1000BC, are located there. The Chamorro people of the Marianas were to develop a distinctive culture as growers of rice, the only cereal raised in ancient times on any of the Pacific islands.

The western lands often traced kinship through the female line (as did some parts of Melanesia). Villages were linked in wider social units known to anthropologists as "matriclans". Although the arrangement gave women influence in group affairs, chiefs were still generally male.

Eastern Micronesian people spoke tongues allied to those of Melanesia's Solomon Islands and

Disruption

Sadly, the myths of Micronesia have mostly been lost as a result of the disruption caused by European contact. Those that survive also show similarities with Polynesian traditions, though there are fewer creation and origin stories and more in the way of trickster tales. In historical times at least, the narratives seem to have served more as entertainment than for any deeper religious purpose. Some story-cycles were quasi-historical, telling of the coming of conquerors from across the sea, and so helping to explain the existing social order.

The Solomon Islanders practised headhunting and when one of their number died they preserved the long bones and the skull of the deceased. It was believed the skull contained the individual's power and it was placed in a small cavity of the fish-shaped reliquaries they built. This example is from Santa Ana Island in the Solomons, collected in the 19th century by a Royal Navy expedition from HMS *Royalist*.

The Pacific Adventurers

Culturally, Polynesia is very much of a piece with Micronesia. The easternmost of the three groups of islands, it forms a triangle with sides roughly 6,500 kilometres long and its corners are Hawaii, Easter Island and New Zealand. Amazingly, this vast area was settled by a single people whose ancestors spread out from Tonga and Samoa after 1300BC.

In the words of the great English navigator Captain James Cook, who explored much of the area: "It is extraordinary that the same nation should have spread themselves over all the isles in this vast ocean, which is almost a fourth part of the circumference of the globe."

The group involved were the Lapita-ware Austronesians, and in the course of two millennia they were to colonize the entire area up to and including Easter Island, more than 2,000 kilometres from the nearest land. Their achievement made them the most widely dispersed people on Earth up to the start of the modern era, and they managed it with no metal and only simple stone tools. Their mode of transport was the outrigger canoe,

which they adapted for long-distance use by lashing two hulls together side by side.

It used to be thought that many of the islands must have been discovered as a result of so-called "drift voyages", in which boats were carried across the ocean at the whim of the tides. Computer simulations discredit this: the predominant currents in the region actually flow westwards, against the movement of settlement. Further vindication of the Polynesians' seafaring skills was supplied in 1976, when a double-canoe crewed by islanders successfully journeyed from Hawaii to Tahiti using only traditional methods of navigation.

It now seems likely that the Polynesians had the maritime expertise necessary to make two-way

TIMELINE	65,000–27,000BC	27,000BC–AD1000

The vast region of Australasia and Oceania is home to a diverse array of cultures, including, in Australia, what might well be the oldest human culture still continuously in existence. The arrival of European explorers from the sixteenth century onwards marked the beginning of a steep decline in indigenous fortunes and beliefs in the face of concerted colonization and culturally destructive activity by Christian missionaries.

*c.*65,000BC Prehistoric remains seem to confirm the existence of early human life in Australia.
*c.*40,000BC Early, tool-using humans lived on the Huon peninsula in what is now New Guinea.
*c.*35,000BC Humans lived in Tasmania.
*c.*31,000BC Early humans settled in the Bismarck Archipelago.
*c.*27,000BC Solomon Islands settled.

A prehistoric carved rock figure from Enga in the Western Highlands of New Guinea. The subject of the so-called Ambum Stone is unknown but may be a spiny anteater's head combined with a human body.

*c.*9000BC A further period of global warming raised sea levels and cut off Tasmania from the mainland and Australia from New Guinea. Cultivation had already begun in New Guinea.
*c.*1300BC Earliest Lapita pottery from the Bismarck Archipelago dates to this period.
*c.*1300–1000BC Lapita Culture expanded through island Melanesia.
*c.*1300BC Eastern Melanesia settled.
*c.*1000BC Micronesia colonized.
*c.*200BC The Marquesas Islands settled.
*c.*50BC Marshall Islands colonized.
*c.*AD300–500 Humans settled on Hawaii and Easter Island.
*c.*500 Stone enclosures built on sites in New Caledonia.
*c.*600 Earliest evidence of human settlement in the Society Islands.
*c.*800–1000 Maori people arrived in Aotearoa (The Land of the Long White Cloud), later to become New Zealand, possibly from the Society Islands. Cook Islands were settled at the same time.
*c.*950 Tui Tonga dynasty established.

exploratory voyages to uninhabited islands before sending out settlers to colonize them. Even so, the long sea voyages must have been desperate undertakings, perhaps only to be contemplated in times of political upheaval, famine or war. The magnitude of the achievement is hardly lessened by simulation studies that indicate that only ten journeys of over 1,000 kilometres into unoccupied waters would have been needed to populate the entire region. Europeans, with the aid of vastly more sophisticated equipment, took 300 years to chart Polynesia accurately after first discovering it in the early sixteenth century.

One thing that is certain is that the incomers were happy with their new home. The 850-kilometre gap from Fiji to the rest of Melanesia effectively acted as a door shutting them off from where they had originally come. In the empty lands of Polynesia they were to develop their own culture, and links with the western islands were largely dropped, although Polynesian influences did filter back.

Maori canoes were *tapu* or sacred space and very often took as their theme the separation of the Earth and sky. The canoe prow shown below has been decorated with intricate spirals which represent light and knowledge coming into the world.

1000–1600

***c.*1000–1600** Estimated time period for the construction of the monumental statues or *ahu* on Easter Island.
***c.*1500** Dutch began to assert control over northern New Guinea.
1521 Ferdinand Magellan landed in Guam on 6 March during his circumnavigation of the world.
1565 Spain claimed the Marianas.
1595–97 Luis Vaez de Torres sailed through the strait between New Guinea and Australia, now named after him.
***c.*1600** Period of highly destructive inter-clan war broke out on Easter Island with building stopped and *ahu* toppled.

A rock-art image in Australia of a European vessel, possibly a river paddle steamer from the 19th century.

1600–1840

1642–43 Abel Janszoon Tasman visited New Ireland.
1668 Spanish missionaries began work in the Marianas.
1768 Bougainville visited Tahiti.
1769–80 James Cook made three voyages to map, explore and scientifically study the Pacific region. On the third trip in 1779 he was killed in Hawaii.
1788 English penal colony established in Australia.
1797 London Missionary Society members settled in the Society and Marquesas islands.
1810–20 Kamehameha I became ruler of Hawaii. Kamehameha II overthrew the *tapu* system and brought in American missionaries.
1840 New Zealand annexed by the UK.

1840–Present Day

A Maori gives the traditional haka *greeting to Queen Elizabeth II during a royal visit.*

1840 British settlers and the Maori signed the Treaty of Waitangi.
1862 Slavers from Peru arrived on Easter Island, reducing the population to 110 by 1877.
1893–1900 US merchants overthrew the Hawaiian queen; US annexed the islands in 1900.
1959 Hawaii given US statehood.
1962–80 Western Samoa, Fiji, Papua New Guinea, Nauru, the Solomon Islands, Kiribati and Vanuatu all gain their independence.
1989 Hawaiian movement formed to reassert indigenous sovereignty.
1992 The Mabo judgement overturned *terra nullius* and acknowledged Aboriginal prior ownership of Australia.

A distinctive feature of the society they created, at least on the larger, more crowded islands, was its rigid social stratification. The community was divided into clans tracing their descent back to venerated common ancestors. Status depended on the closeness of the link, and at birth people were ranked as aristocrats or commoners accordingly.

This hierarchical system drew additional strength from the concept of *mana*, which became highly developed in Polynesia. Emanating originally from the gods, *mana* devolved onto the chiefs who ruled in their name, making everything about them sacred. Contact with *mana* could be physically hazardous for those without the same spiritual radiance, so to limit the danger the persons and presence of the rulers became hedged around by the ritual prohibitions known as *tapu*, the origin of the Western term "taboo".

The result on some islands was an extraordinary despotism. In Tahiti, chiefs were carried on the backs of retainers, and any commoner's house that they entered subsequently had to be burned;

it was *tapu* even to mention the headman's name. In Tonga, Cook saw commoners stooping to touch the sole of a chief's foot as he passed, while in Hawaii subjects could be put to death for failing to prostrate themselves before their sovereign.

The smaller islands had less divided societies, though they too could be far from the tropical paradises that distant Westerners would one day imagine. Their limited economies meant that they were always susceptible to population pressures, and the only options when resources ran out were starvation, warfare or journeys into the unknown.

Some such calamity seems to have afflicted Easter Island, the remotest of them all. The monumental stone heads for which it is famous were

The mysterious stone figures of Easter Island or Rapanui. Their massive-block construction seems to show the influence of Inca techniques and might indicate contact of some sort with Andean civilizations. Intriguingly, the Andean sweet potato was present in the Polynesian islands before the time of European contact, further suggesting such links.

constructed between 1000 and 1600AD. Taking into account the work involved in raising them, one commentator has estimated that 10,000 people must have inhabited the twenty-five-kilometre-long dot of land at that time.

Then something evidently went wrong. The absence of tree cover on the island when Europeans arrived a century later suggests that the sheer number of people may have out-stripped the island's productive capac-ity, and that environmental degradation set in. War followed, with native tradi-tions telling of a conflict that broke out around the year 1680. Thereafter the population fragmented into warring clans locked in combat over a diminish-ing stock of resources. The coup de grace came in 1862, when slavers arrived from Peru to round up the surviving able-bodied male popula-tion; by 1877 there were only 110 individuals left alive.

Something similar happened in New Zealand, though on a less catastrophic scale. The largest of the Polynesian nations, accounting for half of the total landmass of the whole region, it was also the last to be settled. Its Maori inhabi-tants arrived sometime between 800 and 1000AD, making it the last sizeable territory to be peopled on Earth.

Initially it offered huge attractions for the newcomers. Its long isolation had encouraged the evolution of several species of flightless birds that had flourished in the absence of native predators, among them moas twice the size of ostriches. The creatures were easy prey for hunters, providing an abundant supply of fresh meat. Encouraged by this natural bounty, the human population multiplied, reaching a peak by the fourteenth century.

By that time, though, the good times were coming to an end. The moa had been hunted to

Distinctive oversized eyes and a grimacing mouth mark a Hawaiian feather god figure. The large head and crest emphasize its *mana*.

the point of extinction and the popula-tion of the South Island, where the cold climate ruled out much in the way of cultivation, particularly felt the effects. In the North Island people started building fortified strongholds known as *pa* to pro-tect scarce food stocks, especially sweet potatoes which could be stored in pits against times of want. About 5,000 *pa* are thought to have been constructed, indicating that warfare had become endemic.

Meanwhile another cloud had appeared on the horizon that in time was to darken the whole Oceanian world. European navigators had made their way into southern waters. The first to appear was Ferdinand Magellan; his epoch-making circumnavigation of the world took him through the Pacific, and he reached the island of Guam in the Marianas on 6 March 1521.

Many more explorers came in his wake, followed by the colonists. The coming of the white man had a momentous impact on these ancient peoples and for many it proved a calamity, destroying their cultures and leaving only despon-dency and despair in their place. Others came to terms with the new ways, adjusting their customs to take account of the changed situation without losing touch with their own traditions.

And a vital part of that heritage was the cor-pus of myth. Whether local in focus or with wider cosmological overtones, the tales were the way in which hundreds of generations explained their own existence. For millennia, they provided the framework of understanding through which indi-viduals came to terms with their own history and social structure and with the natural world. In the past, they were maps to the unknown; and for many of the region's inhabitants they still form an indispensable element of their identity today.

A TIMELESS LAND

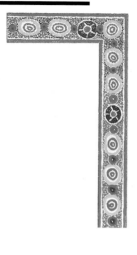

In 1936, during a field trip among central Australia's Warlpiri people, the eminent anthropologist Olive Pink was taken seriously ill. Hundreds of kilometres from a settlement, she was entirely dependent on the Aborigines for her care. Without a driver, her car had to be abandoned. Instead, the Warlpiri made a stretcher from saplings and knotted vine, and carried her through the bush. Their journey took them across some of the harshest territory on Earth, and through millennia of Aboriginal history. When they came to the time-honoured watering places, they scratched holes in the earth from which water promptly flowed and then they prepared a fortifying feast. Her strength restored, the scholar was soon well enough to be taken to the white-run mine at Mount Doreen.

Opposite: **The Bungle Bungle Ranges, in Purnululu territory, epitomize the timeless Australian landscape, having eroded from mountainous sandstone deposits some 350 million years ago.**

Mrs Pink was eventually cured and her experiences and observations were written up, making a valued contribution to understanding in a still-neglected area. But not only did her adventures become part of the academic record, they also passed into the body of Aboriginal myth. The tale of the white woman who fell ill so far from her own kind is still told today by Warlpiri story-tellers, alongside those of heroic battles and fearful monsters, of the ancestors and the creation of the world.

A unique body of living myth, the oral stories of Australia's Aborigines record what in Western historical terms would count as yesterday's news alongside events which took place many thousands of years in the past – from the great floods that followed the end of the last Ice Age to the eruption of volcanoes which have lain dormant for centuries. For all that occurs in their land becomes a part of the land itself; not time but space is the continuum in which history is measured. No external creator conjured this reality into being; the land is the beginning and end of all. "Creation", in this scheme of things, merely moulds what was already there: the idea that the land might once not have existed seems quite simply unimaginable. From a rock formation to a tree, everything extant is seen as a feature of that land; all beings, from an eagle to an anthropologist, have their place in a landscape which exists as much in the spiritual plane as in the physical. Mythology, far more than a set of stories, is a living part of the consciousness by which their universe is mapped; more than this, indeed, it helps construct the Aboriginal sense of self.

Above: **Incised shell pubic shield decorated with inspirational animal figures from the Dreamtime, including reptiles, amphibians, a fish and an emu.**

23

Dreaming the Earth

That heroic time in which the land and its inhabitants were dreamed out of the shapeless earth, thrown up in an explosion of ancestral spirit energy, can also be wandered by the dreamer in the modern here and now.

Arcing and tensing in the infinity of its secret strength, the vast serpent sent a shockwave through the earth. Aroused from endless slumber by some mysterious and intimate signal, it flexed its whole length as it struggled towards wakefulness. Thrusting forwards, tongue flickering and fangs flashing, it exploded upwards through what till that moment had been the blank surface of the world. As rocks and debris showered to the far horizon, the serpent writhed on, bestowing rugged shape on what had been empty indeterminacy. Each corkscrewing twist carved out a valley in the crumbling, quaking earth; every lash of the tail threw up a mountain or a range of hills. Across the entire Australian continent similar serpents were on the move, gouging out deep ravines and pushing up ridges as they went. The ultimate ancestors of the Aboriginal people, these spirits were giving form to a formless world, grinding out the landscape their descendants would inhabit to this day. Other spirits flew down from the heavens to range what had been the smooth surface of the Earth, making all things and giving them their appointed names. They established the different peoples in their allotted lands and gave them their distinct languages, laws and customs.

Such was the violent confusion which conferred order on the Aboriginal world, the incredible cataclysm on which was founded much stability. For the essence of the Aborigine people's existence is its timeless, unchanging mythical and artistic tradition which reinforces the sense of living the same life, in the same landscape, as their forbears. An Aboriginal person knows every metre of his ancestral territory, bleak and monotonous as it might appear to the untutored Western eye. The scrubbiest bush, the barest rock has its established

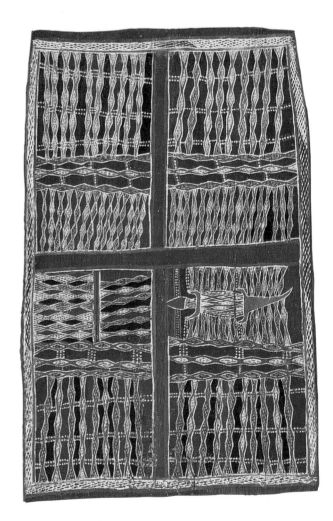

A bark painting from Arnhem Land depicts the story of the Dreaming Crocodile at Ngalawi. The crocodile and other mythic men had made a sacred hut (represented by the cross) at Blue Mud Bay to store their *rangga* emblems while they danced, but it caught fire and Crocodile had to cover himself with lily grass for protection from the flames.

significance for him; no trickling spring is too puny to escape his notice. Set the Aborigine down far from his native haunts, and his internal compass remains exact; he knows his own land in its every detail. Yet he sees it, not objectively, as external to himself, but as part of a whole of which he himself is another part. Myths such as those of the *Altjeringa* or "Dreamtime" help to explain the world in these terms, symbolizing the interconnectedness of humanity and nature.

The Dreamtime

The Dreamtime was that moment when the world first came convulsively into being, thrown up in an explosion of energy by ancestral spirits. As much a metaphysical dimension as a cosmological epoch, however, it endured – indeed still endures – as an ecstatic state open to all who would participate. With the right rituals and incantations the Aborigines can gain access to that same primal spark which first quickened the Earth and has since stirred all their forbears into life. Time is abolished on the instant, in that moment of

enlightenment and energy when the Aborigines connect directly with their own creation. An elaborate mythology handed down orally, from generation to generation, helps to maintain the sense that past and present are one.

So strong is the Aborigine peoples' identification with their ancestors that it matches their sense of individual selfhood: they feel they are essentially the same people, from age to passing age. Timeless myths seem to set the same community within the same natural scene, each rehearsal incorporating new events into the same apparently unchanging schema.

The boundaries which Westerners have so painstakingly erected down the millennia to separate themselves from the natural world have never existed in the minds of Aboriginal peoples. Here all – men, women, animals and every living thing – have been called into being by the same sublime and unceasing dream.

Sacred Energy: The Power of *Djang*

The force the ancestors left latent within the earth is accessible to their descendants in the form of djang, a type of stored-up primal power which collects in certain sacred places.

Held in a particular tree or rock, for instance, this power might be released at a word or a touch to instil strength or confer cunning on the initiate, or to bring much-needed sunshine or rain.

The creative energy by which the world was originally formed, *djang* is literally as old as the hills. The Dreamtime stories tell how spirit beings metamorphosed into things which remain in the landscape. *Djang*'s continued presence allows Aborigines to tap into their people's whole spiritual resource at an instant's notice. *Djang* can also be evoked by the

rituals and dances which reunite the people with the ancestors who inaugurated them.

This gum tree, so distinct in its bare surroundings, is the sort of feature likely to hold supernatural *djang*.

Shaping the Contours

That dream resonates too in the land-scape's every rugged contour, criss-crossed as it was in the primal Dreamtime by the originating spirits. In the shape not only of giant snakes but of bounding kangaroos or wallabies, scuttling lizards or creeping crocodiles, the ancestral heroes traversed throughout their terrain, establishing order and inaugurating tribes. The two goanna, or monitor, men, for instance, roamed the length and breadth of what is today called the Great Victoria Desert, creating its animals and plants and performing its founding rituals. In the course of their travels, it is reported, they met with other important spirits: the Opossum Woman, the Moon Man and the Mountain Devil. The Djanggawul brother and sisters emerged from the eastern sea in the wake of the rising sun to pace out the northern coastline of the continent. As they went they gave birth to peoples, whom they endowed with eternal rites, finally following the setting sun into the western ocean where they sank gently beneath the waves. Another establisher of the tropical north, Tor Rock, can be seen to this very day. Now no more than a geological feature of the Arnhem Land coast he once helped to furnish with animals, plants and men, he remains a potent spirit in the mind of the area's indigenous inhabitants.

Wherever they went these wayfaring spirits marked out the places where they had camped or hunted with features such as caves, creeks or rivers, gleaming saltpans or clumps of trees. Every rock, every dried-up streambed they endowed with sacred significance for all time to come. Sometimes the routes the spirits

In art as in myth and landscape, the Dreaming was the single subject in which all creation was contained. Spoken stories were captured visually in an art which reflected the fluid interaction between human spirit figures and animal heroes, such as those seen here.

Reading the Landscape

The "dreaming tracks" the ancestral spirits followed in their originating journeys across the Australian land have an equivalent in the "song lines" they left behind, connecting the sacred sites.

Audible only to the initiate, "song lines" are stories encoded in the landscape: a tribe's whole history and culture is there for those with eyes to read or with ears to hear. If the Aborigines see their world as essentially static and stable, they for their part are always on the move – not only as hunter-gatherers but as part of their religious observance. Although a big part of their ritual takes the form of collective ceremonies and dancing, the personal pilgrimage is important too. Far from wandering idly and aimlessly the Aborigine on "walkabout" retraces the steps of his ancestors, following "song lines" and "dreaming tracks" in a strenuous bid to ingest the energy and history of his forbears from the dawn of time.

Much Aboriginal knowledge is secret. These boys are being initiated along their tribe's "song line" path – the sacred drawings can only be seen later.

followed were many hundreds of kilometres long, making paths that might figure in the mythologies of many different peoples; others went on just a few kilometres and were known only to a number of local tribes. However long or short, though, the routes of their wanderings have remained sanctified in Aboriginal tradition. The spirit's original life-force remains eternally present along these paths, available countless generations on to the initiate in his secret cult. By striking a stone upon which the spirit rested or rubbing the spot at which he entered or emerged from the earth, the Aborigine can draw upon his ancestor's primal energy for strength and skill in hunting or in war.

Much of southwestern Australia was created by a watersnake, the Wagyal, who possessed both masculine and feminine forms, and was simultaneously one and many. Creating mountains, lakes and rivers, such as the Swan on which Perth would one day be sited, his/her form is still discernible in the long escarpment visible from the modern city. A derelict brewery now stands on the site where the Wagyal settled down to lay her eggs: for thousands of years, Aboriginal women from the region would journey to this sacred spot when their time came to give birth. Those born at such sacred places are entrusted with their care and protection: they are, it is said, not just descendants but reincarnations of the ancestral being. Other spirits took up residence within particular birds, animals and insects – honoured still by their Aboriginal descendants, for whom they are important totemic figures (see pages 54–57).

Etched into a rock face, an Aboriginal image becomes part of the very creation it represents; painted in pigments ground up from ashes, earth and bark, it partakes of the natural order it sets out to depict. That such creations tend subsequently to be seen as the work not of human but of spirit artists only underlines the continuity they affirm. So too does the fact that the same stories are painted on the bodies of Aborigines for sacred rituals which help commemorate and celebrate their oneness with the Earth. The great corroborees, or tribal assemblies, at which complicated dances are performed and elaborate rituals staged, recall earlier spirit conventions during the Dreamtime, back at the beginning when the world was being made.

A Deluge of Destruction

The story of the Dreamtime flood that engulfed the existing world and established a new one is central to the mythology of many northern Aboriginal tribes whose homelands were far wetter and lusher than those found in the desert interior.

While many Aboriginal peoples believe that the world they inhabit was born of great upheavals in the entrails of the Earth, some see its origins in a mighty deluge. They hold that a great flood swept away a prior creation to clear the way for the world we see about us today. This alternative origin myth is particularly prevalent among peoples who inhabit the tropical north – such as the Murinbata, who live in today's Northern Territory. The destructive – and creative – power of the sea would of course be well known to dwellers in Australia's coastal regions in a way it could not possibly be to those who lived in the continent's arid interior.

As it happens, archaeological evidence seems to support the theory that these northern areas were indeed subject to fearful floods in the temperate aftermath of the last Ice Age. The dramatic rise in sea levels that resulted when the ice caps finally thawed brought about large-scale inundations in coastal areas worldwide. The societies of northern Australia seem to have been particularly badly affected – the effects can be discerned in everything from settlement patterns to rock art. The myth of a cataclysmic worldwide flood is believed by scholars to have originated at about the same time as the post-glacial changes stabilized themselves to mark out the Australian shoreline at its present level.

An Aboriginal depiction of a Wandjina rain spirit. The term is a generic one from the Kimberley region for those spirits controlling the elements and fertility.

The thawing of far-distant ice sheets could not of course be expected to figure in the Aborigines' own account of this catastrophe. Looking for causes much closer to hand, their storytellers attributed the flood to a variety of human and animal spirits. For the Worora of the Kimberley region, the floods were the ruthless work of their ancestral spirits, the Wandjina, who wanted the whole world as it was to be swept away to make room for a new one where they and their descendants could live and thrive. As the waters subsided, the Wandjina split up and spread out to settle in every part of their newly established world. Their separate territories marked out by their distinctive rock paintings, theirs was a whole new creation, its predecessor quite forgotten.

Karen, the Bird-man Totem

It rained and rained, said the Murinbata storyteller, and the water rose higher and higher. The face of the world was initially changed, then progressively erased, as first the valley bottoms, then the low-lying plains were drowned. The thorny scrub, then the forest tree-tops disappeared beneath the steadily rising water; where once there had been hills there was now a spreading sea. Rivers and streams lost their way now the land lay under water: with no banks or rocky ravines to guide them, they had no idea where to flow. Soon the earth had almost completely disappeared beneath the rising ocean, only a solitary mountaintop peeping out from the lapping waves.

To its increasingly crowded summit those spirits who had survived the cataclysm made their fearful way. Led thither by the stone-curlew man, Karen, the men of the bird-totems were the first to arrive. They could fly above the waters with ease – but still needed somewhere to set down and roost when nightfall came. They were soon joined by those animal totems who had managed to swim to sanctuary there, bringing with them food and supplies as if for a siege. Working together in a frenzy of activity, they built a bulwark of stones around their island retreat. They looked on fearfully as the waters rose still higher, threatening to overspill their barrier and engulf this last outpost of dry land. With relief, they saw that it was holding; and in time the torrential rainstorms slackened and then stopped.

As they gazed at the endless sea around them, they wondered whether the waters might not at last have started to subside, but the first bird-men Karen sent out to investigate came back without having caught any glimpse of land. Not long after, however, Karen sent two honey-eater men; they were gone a whole day and night, and their friends were beginning to fear for their safety, when they appeared winging their way across the waters clutching leafy branches in their beaks. The flood still covered most of the world, it seemed, but the crisis had undoubtedly passed. As the waters ebbed away the surviving spirits stepped tentatively forth into a new and empty world; dispersing in all directions they established new nations in every part of the land. Karen, the leader who had brought the Aboriginal ancestors to their new world, did not stay with them to enjoy it. Instead he flew up high into the sky to give thanks for their safe deliverance. Higher and higher he soared until finally he had reached the level of the moon, then he turned into a twinkling star and took up residence in the heavens for ever.

The Thrush and the Flood

It was thanks to Kaboka the thrush that Victoria's Tambo River first flooded. He went hunting one day in the Dreamtime, with wretched results.

When he returned to camp at day's end, there was no sign of the rich bag he and his friends had all hoped for: Kaboka had only a single, scrawny wallaby. Still, he made ready to cook it and share it just the same. But his companions scorned his offering, complaining about such a meagre meal. Tired from his long day and angered by their ingratitude, the thrush took the food back and told them to catch their own. Furious, he lit a sacred fire, and danced round it for hours until he had raised a storm of terrible winds and torrential rain. He danced on and the rain kept falling down until the whole country was awash and his companions were all drowned. When the Tambo floods today, it is due to Kaboka remembering his day of rage.

The Serpent and the Rainbow

Water was believed to have been created by the ancestral spirits when the world came into being. The Rainbow Snake, oldest and most universal of the Aboriginal spirit identities, symbolized the water without which life could not continue.

His feet were tough and leathery enough to take the most jagged stones in their stride, and yet the boy winced none the less at the temperature of the rocks he was walking across. Accustomed as he was to the stifling heat of the dry season, he still found himself seized by something approaching panic for a moment as his lungs heaved on the searing desert air. As the twigs crackled, dry and brittle beneath his feet, his nerves seemed only a hair's breadth away from snapping too. All in this arid landscape seemed on the point of burning up: the boy was no exception. Increasingly bored and irritable back in the camp, he had come out here to kill an afternoon, yet the feeling of being slowly cooked was doing nothing whatever for his mood.

As far as the eye could see the sky was an uninterrupted expanse of blue; from horizon to farthest horizon, not a single cloud could be seen. No rain had fallen for weeks; had it really ever rained at all? Moisture was no more than a memory here – or worse, it was a tantalizing mirage, like the heat haze that ringed the sun or the vast lake that seemed to shimmer in the valley bottom: mocking parodies of the water for which all nature was so palpably athirst. Suddenly the boy stood stock still, transfixed by the sight of a snake making its way across a boulder before him, trickling

A waterhole in the Northern Territory's lush and tropical Kakadu National Park. Water, the source of all life, was the gift of the ancestral spirits at the beginning of the world. Some waterholes are sacred and Aboriginal clans act as their custodians; others can be therapeutic or dangerous. The serpent symbolized the wet season and the replenishment of the water.

like liquid over the dry face of the solid stone. In its winding and unravelling coils he could see the meandering of a river; in its lithe languidness he sensed a terrible energy waiting to be unleashed. Most of all, in its inscrutable beauty he felt the presence of unimaginable power: in this mysterious phallic form could be contained all the potency of the world, all the surging strength of water and its capacity to destroy and to save.

The Symbolism of the Snake

The never-ending quest for water in arid conditions defines the rhythm of existence for many Aboriginal peoples; only in the tropical north and temperate south can a ready supply be taken for granted. At the mundane level, the people have a strong positive sense of water's importance, yet they are under no illusions about its immense destructive power. At a more spiritual level, the

Taipan, the Shaman-snake

Among the Wik Kalkan of the Cape York Peninsula, the story of the snake-deity Taipan is told. Once a man and a powerful magician, he could cure the sick – or kill the healthy – at will.

He could control not only human life and death but the elements: the lightning flashed and the thunder rumbled at his command. For wives he had the watersnakes Uka and Tuknampa, and Mantya the death-adder. Only one child had been born of these alliances, however: a fine son, whom Taipan loved above all things. But one day when the youth went hunting downriver he fell in love with the watersnake Tintauwa, wife of Wala the blue-tongued lizard. She seduced him, and they ran away together into the bush.

Wala gave chase and murdered Taipan's son. The magician was left desolate by his loss. Calling his family together he daubed them all with the blood of his child, before sending them down to take up residence in the earth in whose depths he himself soon joined them. His two sisters,

meanwhile, he sent off to the highest Heaven, telling them to add their nephew's red blood to the other colours of the rainbow. It can be seen there to this day, richest colour in the spectrum of

the arc of life, in which it stands symbolically for the regenerative blood of menstruation.

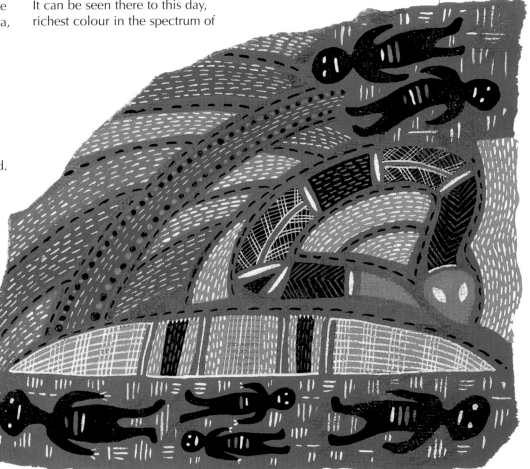

summoning of rain by rituals, and the expression of thanks to those spirits which have delivered it, are central preoccupations of religious life.

All this significance, for good and for evil, is invested symbolically in the figure of the snake, whose bite may bring death and yet whose furious coilings carry a suggestion of the quickening impulse of life at creation's heart; whose slender shape suggests the arcing of the rainbow, with all the fertility contained in the gently dropping rain – and with all the latent destructiveness of downpour and sudden flash flood.

It is therefore scarcely surprising that the Rainbow Snake should be one of the oldest and most ubiquitous of all the Aboriginal ancestral figures. It can be seen represented on rocks and cave walls the length and breadth of the Australian continent; it is heard of in the mythology of just about every Aboriginal tribe; and – most important of all, perhaps – its "dreaming presence" is sensed in every waterhole and winding river, of all of which it is at once both creator and proprietary spirit. The Aborigine would never dream of taking water from a billabong without first ritually asking the Rainbow Snake's permission; no more than he would envisage taking the spirit's fish, animals or waterfowl without its authority either. Told by the Djauan people of Arnhem Land, the tale of the black rock-snake Kurrichalpongo is typical in its evocation of the Rainbow Snake's profound – and profoundly ambivalent – power.

Nagacork and Kurrichalpongo

Old man Nagacork, says the story, had searched vainly upriver and down for the special water-shooting fish which was so rare and so dear to his heart. What was wrong with more common fish? the other men asked him, scooping a rich bounty readily from the stream. Their day's hunting done while his was mired in frustration, they laughed and splashed in the shallows and mocked the earnest single-mindedness of his search.

In time Nagacork came to wonder whether they were not right: he had not seen so much as a scale of the fish he desired – would no other kind really meet his need? Then just as he was despairing of ever finding the water-shooting fish, he saw a column of ants marching up the trunk of a tree. He climbed up to see what they had found, and there, in a hollow cleft, found the blackened bones of the fish he had sought so long and hard. His fellow tribesmen, it seemed, had killed and eaten it, then hidden its bones away from sight. Sadly he climbed down the tree and, seating himself among its roots, he sang a song to the black rock-snake Kurrichalpongo.

The serpent came to his summons, arcing down from the sky, a multi-coloured bow in the heavens above his native northern mountains. Where it entered the ground it bored a hole in the bank of a billabong, releasing a torrent of water which inundated the entire area. Nagacork's impious neighbours were either swept away on the angry torrent or escaped by taking on other forms – those of flying birds, for example, or swimming turtles. Now Kurrichalpongo laid eggs which hatched into baby Rainbow Snakes: in every direction they dispersed, their twisting, coiling forms scraping out rivers and billabongs as they went, while the much bigger Kurrichalpongo carved out what is now the Wilton River.

When the black rock-snake reached Luralingi, on the Hodgson River, he reared high into the air, eyes flashing and tongue flickering. The sky grew black and menacing; a great bolt of lightning cleft the sky and the heavens thundered. The mountains trembled at the terrible sound and a rushing wind broke off tree trunks like twigs; rain fell in torrents and the rising water swept violently downriver in a mighty wave, carrying off everything that lay in its path. The Wallipooroo, the Mara, the Yookul, the Karkaringi: all these tribes, and many more, were destroyed en masse, leaving their lands for the sons of Nagacork, the Djauan. Ever mindful of these violent origins, the Djauan would always treat the Rainbow Snake's power with the utmost respect, seeking its permission before drawing its water or wading into its realm in search of fish or turtles.

Ngalyod, as the Rainbow Snake is called in western Arnhem Land, is depicted here with two horns and a crocodile tail. One local story describes Ngalyod eating an orphan who had attracted its attention by crying. Another tells of three birds, one a pewee, that the snake ate. They pecked a hole from which to escape from its belly, emerging as humans and killing their captor as they did so.

Spirit of the Ancestral Sisters

The phallic power of the Rainbow Snake met an opposing feminine force in one of the great founding myths of Aboriginal culture, society and life. The story of the Wawilak sisters emphasized the complementary nature of male and female.

One day during the deepest Dreamtime, two sisters walked side by side together out of the rolling ocean breakers and stepped, dripping wet, onto the Arnhem Land shore at what is now Trial Bay. The older sister was carrying a small baby slung in a little paperbark cradle; the younger was evidently well advanced in a pregnancy of her own. Each was armed with a long spear, and as they struck north into the interior it became abundantly clear that these were no mere ornaments but tools for active – and skilful – use. Bandicoots, possums and monitors the sisters killed for their food, supplementing this meat with herbs and fruit which they gathered: they named all the different plants and animals as they made their

Carved representations of the two Wawilak, or Wagilag, sisters. The basic elements of this major ancestral story exist in different Aboriginal cultures with the names and small details changed.

leisurely way inland, endowing meaning and form on what till then had been an empty waste.

Suddenly one day the younger sister felt the first contractions which signalled that her time was approaching. Her sister prepared her a bed beside the Mirarrmina waterhole. She set up camp and started a fire and went to fetch food for her labouring sister, but every time she killed an animal and tried to cook it, it simply leaped up from the flames and jumped plop into the pool.

What the women did not realize was that Yulunggur, the Rainbow Snake, lay slumbering beneath the surface of the water. He – for his power was masculine – was the billabong's resident spirit and the owner of all the district's game; no one else had any business, it seemed, taking what belonged to him. Still oblivious, however, to what was going on just a few metres away on the bank beside him, the serpent dozed on unheeding – until the moment when the older sister pursued a fleeing creature to the water's edge. She was menstruating at that time, as it happened, and as she stepped into the shallows, a drop of blood fell into the water and roused the angry serpent from his sleep. He came surging up from the dark depths, the resulting tidal wave flooding the earth; he towered up on his tail and struck furiously at the sky. Then he bore down angrily on the two women who had so violated his privacy. They danced and chanted in the hope of calming his rage, but their efforts were to no avail. Yulunggur spread his jaws wide and swallowed both the sisters and their children; at last, he hoped, he might be left in peace to continue with his sleep. It was not to be, however; awoken themselves by all this turmoil the other snakes started quizzing him about what had been going on. Yulunggur lied, telling his serpent neighbours that he had simply caught and eaten a kangaroo, but not one of them would believe the tale he told. He was finally forced to confess that he had eaten the two women and their children. No sooner had he finished speaking than the monsoon wind blew in: it battered him with its gusting force and with sheets of driving rain. Yulunggur was forced to bow down low before its merciless onslaught; in his agonized thrashings he carved out a river valley, then with a great roar he vomited up the sisters and their children. They fell into a nest of ants, whose angry biting brought them quickly back to life. Yulunngur, meanwhile, crawled ignominiously away, back down to his billabong lair.

The Wawilak sisters are, scholars have suggested, the daughters of the "Old Woman", Kunapipi. As original Earth Mother, this figure represented a rival, feminine claimant to the creative power of the archetypally male Rainbow Snake. In some traditions she seems to have been revered as a pre-eminent ancestor, taking the form either of an old woman or her own daughter, a nubile girl. Mostly, however, the woman and the Rainbow Snake are honoured as a duality, as representatives of those eternal masculine and feminine principles from whose conjunction all life and creativity must spring. The myth of the Wawilak sisters is typical of this tradition, affirming as it does the profound complementarity of the female and the male. In devouring the old woman's offspring the snake takes to himself their great strength and wisdom: from that time forth men, and not women, will be the custodians of tribal learning and law. Yet the victory, it is clear, is by no means entirely with Yulunggur: he can neither match the women's fertility nor withstand the life-giving abundance of the monsoon rain. Vomited forth from the belly of the serpent, the women are restored to life, and their spirit lives on side by side with his. But where the snake's form can be seen as signifying the male organ, the old woman and her child-bearing daughters represent the productive womb. Both masculine and feminine principles are essential to the continuation of human life: there is a place for both serpent and sisters in the Aboriginal mythic scheme.

The sisters' story forms an important part of Dhuwa ceremonies. This interpretation of the story shows the richness of plants and animals surrounding the Rainbow Snake, which is coiled to represent the Mirarrmina waterhole.

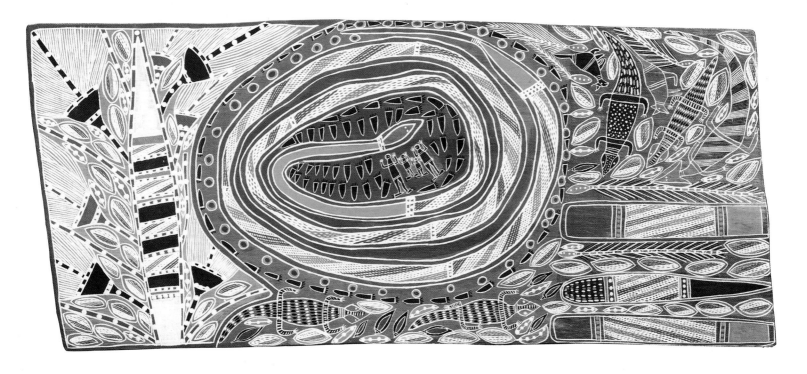

Creator of Bounty and Abundance

Some Aboriginal peoples revere supreme, "all-father" figures: Ngurunderi, of southeastern Australia, is one of the best known of these. Although immensely influential he was not all-powerful, remaining vulnerable in a very human way.

Just as the Murray River is on the point of concluding its long journey, the waterway widens abruptly, its sweeping current suddenly slowing, the broad expanse of Lake Alexandrina barring the way to the open sea. Along the shores of this great lake fishermen have clustered since time immemorial, drawn by the incredible harvest of fish and seafood to be garnered there. Both the fish in the lake itself and all the riches of the sea just a short way downstream: no fisherman could want more than this – not only great abundance but variety. It is hard to imagine a time when this bustling estuary was not crowded. But in fact, insist the elders of the local Jaraldi people, this greatest of Australia's waterways was once no more than a muddy trickle. Only land animals roamed these open flatlands in the days when the world was young; only the tiniest stream threaded its solitary way across the infinite monotony of the plain. As for the nearby sea, it was empty and lifeless, just as the Earth itself had been millennia before.

Ngurunderi, they say, was the ancestral spirit who changed all that, making bounty and abundance where once was bleakness. More ambitious in their creative scope than other ancestors or totem spirits, and more consistent in their continuing protectiveness towards their tribe, Ngurunderi, and other "all-fathers" like him, are the nearest the Aboriginal pantheon comes to a quasi-Christian divinity. It has been suggested by some scholars that such spirits arose under the influence of the first European missionaries' teaching. The Jaraldi's Ngurunderi has equivalents in certain other Aboriginal cultures of the region: most notable of these is Biame, who first made the animals as practice for creating humankind.

But while these spirits may have been "all-fathers", they were certainly not all-powerful in the Judaeo-Christian way. With all his great strength and wisdom and his immense influence upon the world, Ngurunderi still seems a profoundly vulnerable man. A solitary figure whose wives had long-since abandoned him, taking with them his beloved children, he led a lonely life hunting in the hills inland. He never thought to come down to the coast, for what should he expect to find there? No food could be caught in the sterile sea.

But one day Ngurunderi was drawn out of his way, when a giant Murray cod he had started

Milapukala, the All-Mother

Much of Bathurst Island was the creation of a cockatoo-woman. Near the place where she camped at the island's southeastern corner, she caused a large freshwater lagoon to be formed.

She had it hemmed in by rocky headlands for protection, and placed a fertile plain on its landward side. Into the rich and varied environment she had so lovingly created, she commanded all manner of animal and plant life to come.

The people who lived in this place would thus always be assured of an abundance of food, bequeathed to them by their creator and "all-mother".

Now a cleft rock on the shore of her lagoon, the cockatoo-woman still watches over her people. They gather there every year to celebrate her achievement. Their festivities, it is felt, do not merely honour and commemorate Milapukala but continue her work, magically increasing the stock of plants and animals in her little world.

trailing far upriver began making its way south-wards towards the sea. A huge monster of a fish, determined to escape its pursuer at any price, it was undeterred by the size of the little stream. Thrashing its tail and leaping in its eagerness to escape its persecutor, its fevered heavings gouged out the modern Murray River. Reaching the widening waters of Lake Alexandrina it felt suddenly liberated and charged straight for the open sea. Ngurunderi could only look on in bitter disappointment as he watched it disappear into the distance. But then, just as it seemed inevitable that his hard-hunted quarry was going to escape him at the last, he remembered his brother-in-law, Nepele, who lived further down the river.

Alerted then by Ngurunderi's cries, Nepele speared the monster as it passed. The two men then cut their catch into little pieces, and scattered them on the water before them: each promptly took on the form of a new fish species. Some swam off upriver; others set off down to the sea: by the time Ngurunderi and Nepele were done, they had created every freshwater and saltwater fish imaginable. A large hunk of the monster was left; that, the men decided, would be the cod itself: king of all the fish, whether of roaring ocean or of running river. From that time forth the sea seethed with life, while the rivers and streams were full of fish of their own, a vital resource for countless communities of Aboriginal people down the generations.

This bark painting represents the story of the Dreaming Barramundi fish which shares many similarities with the Ngurunderi tale. Although speared, the fish escaped and made for the sea, turning itself into a rock at the mouth of the river.

The Melatji Law Dogs

In the apparently commonplace tale of two dingoes looking for water can be read lessons of far weightier significance concerned with the peaceful coexistence of both individuals and entire peoples, as well as a reflection of the respect felt by Aboriginals for the dogs.

The dingo was held in special regard by Aboriginal people. Serving as a pet and a hunting aid, it embodied tribal law and bore a godlike spirit in the form of the Melatji Law Dogs. This rock painting of the two dogs is from caves in the Napier Range of the remote northwest Kimberley region.

Pushing south across the continent's arid interior, the two dingoes cast about for water as they went. Every so often, one or the other would stop and scratch frantically at the soil; water would well up from the arid earth at that point, another billabong inaugurated for all time to come. Never following a simple straight line but always skittering back and forth, quartering the landscape in their ranging, questing run, the dingoes opened up all of Australia in this way, establishing a network of life-giving waterholes and connecting trails.

The myths say that these first dingoes came from far away across the northern ocean. (Interestingly, modern zoological science agrees that they may indeed have made their way to the continent by sea some 5,000 years ago.) The "Melatji Law Dogs" are said to have made their first landfall in the territory of the Bunuba people, at what is now King Sound on the Kimberley coast.

Their progress through Bunuba lands amounts to nothing less than a mythological map of that country's real water resources. As they dug in the sand the dogs threw up the King Leopold Mountains, before heading south to Fitzroy Crossing and then striking westwards to the Windjana Gorge where they imprinted themselves on a rock.

The Milk of Knowledge

As is the way with the myths of the Aboriginal peoples, the same figures occur in many different communities, although each group knows only that part of the story which concerns itself. In the deserts of central Australia the dingo spirits milked the blind snake spirit Jarapiri of all his knowledge. These treasures included stories, sacred songs, hunting techniques, tools, ceremonies and the laws by which humanity should live.

Fire and Fidelity

The dogs' general role as lawgivers is taken for granted, but the emphasis of the laws embodied may differ considerably from place to place. The Warlpiri tell two stories with different lessons.

The eastern Warlpiri lived abutting other peoples and this influences the tale. The story begins with fire. A basic of human technological life, the campfire is also the social centre around which Aboriginals are born, live and die – the constant in what can be a nomadic lifestyle. The two dogs tried various kindlings without success, until finally they picked on the *ngaljin-ngaljinji* and their fire burst into life almost immediately. This is the wood their Aboriginal descendants have always used since. The dogs ranged far and wide, but wherever they went they found themselves blundering up against other dog peoples, with their own laws, customs, rituals and social integrity. The two had to adjust and make allowances for these. Finally, with a little give and take, they were able to found their own land. Tolerance, cooperation and respect for each other's views enabled the different dog peoples to succeed in coexisting side by side.

The western Warlpiri lived sufficient to themselves. They tell of two dogs who, as elsewhere, created features in the landscape and then parted for a time, he taking a path to the north of the Tapu rock-hole, she branching off to the south. But as he made his way eastwards without his companion, he slowly began to realize just how much he missed her. He howled desolately late into the night. Far to the south she heard his anguished cry and was stirred. Loping north she called to her partner as she ran: they were mates, she knew, made to belong together and live fruitfully. Heading eastwards together they dug out a new waterhole at Larrka: the male fashioned two matrimonial headdresses from the sand there. He put his on, she eagerly donned hers and they were joined as man and wife. They danced and sang, and performed ceremonies. That night for the first time, they lay down as a married couple, a fit model for all such partners ever since.

A regenerative bush fire engulfs a waterhole in Arnhem Land. The water-seeking route that the Melatji Law Dogs traced led to an Aboriginal "mind map" of essential, life-giving waterholes.

The Making of Humankind

From the Arrente of central Australia comes a creation myth in which humanity is shaped from clay. It differs, however, from Western myths where life is formed from the inert earth. The point is that life inheres in the soil; the "creator" merely releases what is already there.

The making of men and women has no part in most Aboriginal traditions; while creation myths loom large, it is with the landscape and the people's spiritual origins that they are mainly concerned. Snakes, dingoes, monitors, kangaroos – the list of animal ancestors is well-nigh endless, but little is said about how men and women first came to take on their present physical form. This lack of curiosity appears strange to those whose cultural background causes them to place humankind instinctively at the centre of the natural world. But so close were the Aborigines to nature that they were able to see themselves as just another part of the landscape.

Shaping Humankind

From high up among the stars the Numbakulla brothers looked down, divine beings of the utmost benevolence and power. Their heavenly perch commanded a sweeping view of the entire Earth, and they watched its infinite emptiness night and day. No human figure moved, for men and women had yet to be formed. But as they scanned and re-scanned the Earth's vast surface to see what secrets it might yet yield, they were suddenly seized by the sense of certain figures taking form. Far below, by a silent saltlake, scoured by a restless wind, a giant boulder cast its shadow across the clammy clay. The brothers' watching gaze was drawn to

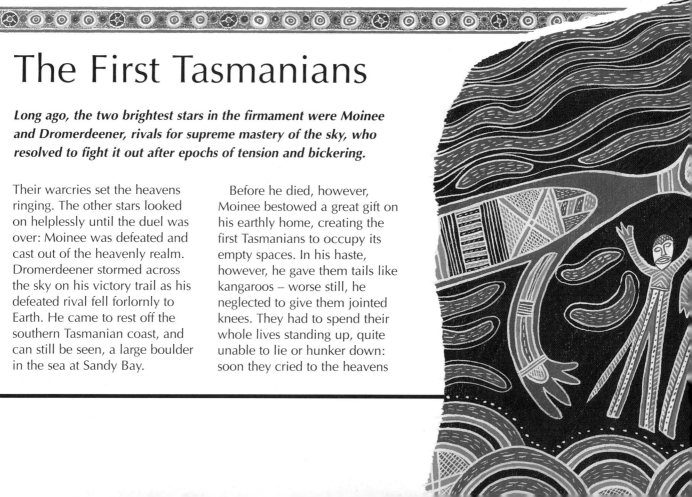

The First Tasmanians

Long ago, the two brightest stars in the firmament were Moinee and Dromerdeener, rivals for supreme mastery of the sky, who resolved to fight it out after epochs of tension and bickering.

Their warcries set the heavens ringing. The other stars looked on helplessly until the duel was over: Moinee was defeated and cast out of the heavenly realm. Dromerdeener stormed across the sky on his victory trail as his defeated rival fell forlornly to Earth. He came to rest off the southern Tasmanian coast, and can still be seen, a large boulder in the sea at Sandy Bay.

Before he died, however, Moinee bestowed a great gift on his earthly home, creating the first Tasmanians to occupy its empty spaces. In his haste, however, he gave them tails like kangaroos – worse still, he neglected to give them jointed knees. They had to spend their whole lives standing up, quite unable to lie or hunker down: soon they cried to the heavens the spot: they looked more closely, at once astonished and appalled. For there in the sticky mud indeterminate half-outlines could be seen; the shapes were so unformed, it was scarcely surprising they had missed them so many times before. Prisoners of the earth, they simply lay there, unmoving, in the mud. Their stumpy limbs were too short and indefinite for them even to swivel on the spot where they lay, far less to venture out into the world. Lacking all power of movement, they were without physical senses too, with no eyes to see, no ears to hear and no mouths to speak. They could have no social contact with one another, no individual will: none of the things, indeed, which we associate with human life.

From their eyrie in the stars, the brothers saw the suffering of these embryonic half-beings and felt compassion. Descending from the heavens, each clutching a stone knife, they landed where these unhappy creatures lay and promptly set

about cutting them free from their muddy bonds. First they shaped their nebulousness into definition, marking out each with a distinct torso and head, the fundamental division of the human body. Then they hacked great Vs to the lower section and to the sides, so that arms and legs might swing loose from the rest. At the end of each extremity they next nicked out little fingers and toes: recognizably human now, the clay beings could stand upright on their own. As yet, however, they could neither hear nor talk, smell nor see: they were still a long way from what we would consider human. The brothers soon saw to that, though, cutting out eyes and mouths with their sharp blades before punching ears and nostrils with their fingers. Finally they fashioned the organs which marked the beings out not merely as people but as male and female: from now on they would be able to reproduce themselves. And so indeed they did, multiplying and spreading out to fill up the land for many days' walking around: the men and women of the Arrente tribe.

to take pity on their plight. Dromerdeener finally heard their call: ruthless though he was, he was moved by what he saw. Descending from Heaven, he chopped off their tails and rubbed healing grease upon the wounds. Then to the middle of each leg he added a hinge-like knee: the people were now free to squat or lie down as they wanted.

Rich Ochres of Parachilna

Prized above all other pigments in the Aboriginal scheme of things, ochre was valued for its artistic and ceremonial uses. Red ochre was the most prestigious of all. A legend claimed that that of Parachilna in the Flinders Range was once the blood of a dying dog.

Just to the north of Adelaide lie the gentle hills of the Flinders Range. Although wild enough to be romantic, nature here is bountiful and benign. While this is rough and stony ground, the landscape is a world away from the sunbaked sand and rock of Australia's austere interior. Nobody now would guess that these hills were once the scene of a vicious fight to the death, yet that is what happened when, on a dark Dreamtime day, one of the Melatji Law Dogs strayed alone into the area.

At that time the Flinders were home to a giant gecko lizard named Adno-artina who guarded his territory jealously. Each day he would climb up to the mountains' topmost peak and bellow forth a challenge to the world. Whoever fought him, and killed him, could claim title to these lands, he said. For many years he went unanswered – for none was so rash as to try his great strength.

One day, however, Marindi passed that way, his dreaming track having brought him to these hills. He heard the gecko's challenge, and knew he must respond. Barking out his defiant reply he went bounding up the valley towards the peak from which Adno-artina looked down in mounting consternation. He had grown used to his challenge going entirely undisputed; he certainly had not expected an enemy as formidable as this. With his great spreading jaws and his long, sharp teeth, the dog was terrifying to behold. The gecko decided to temporize a little while he thought of some ploy by which he might prevail against such a foe. He therefore excused himself from an immediate fight, saying he would take the challenger on later. Marindi saw no reason to object to a short delay, but he warned that he would make the lizard food for his pups. He then curled up at the foot of the mountain and went to sleep. Meanwhile, Adno-

These ancient ochre hand stencils are found in the Blue Mountains in southern Australia. The colour red stood for the element of fire, and additionally its bloody hue was seen as representing *djang* energy.

artina's mind was racing, seeking a strategy to overcome the mighty Marindi. At last he had his plan. As evening gave way to night, he tied a magic hair tight round the root of his tail lest in the forthcoming combat his courage might ebb away into it. Then he crept down from his mountaintop to the level ground beneath and abruptly yelled out his challenge.

Roused suddenly from his sleep, Marindi snapped up at the peak where Adno-artina had been, allowing the gecko to scuttle beneath his guard. The lizard caught him by the throat, and held on just as tightly as he could. In vain did the dog shake and swing him, and try to tear him away with his claws: the gecko hung on grimly while the dog's lifeblood flowed away. It stained the ground permanently on the valley floor, and the resulting red ochre has been prized throughout

Aboriginal history. Although the cunning victor, the gecko bears a scar to this day: a slight constriction round the tail where it meets the body.

Ochres were used both for creating artworks on sand or stone and for ceremonial body-painting. Red ochre was by far the most prestigious of the mineral's various forms: where white ochre was used as a body-pigment for public displays and black ochre for ritual body-scarring, red ochre – symbolizing the blood of ancestors – was reserved for the most secret of ceremonies, such as circumcisions and initiations into manhood.

The Flinders Range was known across much of southern and central Australia as a rich source of all these ochres, though opinions differed as to how they had got there. For the inhabitants of the mountains themselves the figure of Witana loomed large: the giant who had created the hills and gorges among which they lived, he had also established their essential laws and customs. The body-scarring ceremony by which black ochre was rubbed into wounds was said to have been inaugurated by Witana personally.

Once, when camping at Wataku-wadlu in the Flinders Range, Witana was called upon to conduct some initiation ceremonies. Feeling that such a momentous occasion should be marked out in some way, he decided to use his own blood as decoration for the youths' bodies. Taking a knife, he cut deep into his arms, both left and right, and the dark liquid flowed forth, spattering the earth beneath. From one arm the blood ran red: this mixed with the earth to become red ochre. From the other limb it flowed black, staining the rocks upon which it landed and producing a fine reef of black ochre.

The Emu and the Ochre

One day a man walked out with his dogs in the Flinders Range near Parachilna; his wife was nearby, gathering grass seed to grind later. Suddenly both stiffened, startled by rustling from the undergrowth.

Their dogs had disturbed an emu, which now burst forth before their very eyes and fled headlong in terror. Over hills and mountains the bird ran, the dogs in hot pursuit, fording rivers, leaping streams, bursting through thickets and scrambling over rocks. Slowly, the dogs were gaining, while their quarry visibly tired: at the final moment, however, they would be cheated of their prey. The emu ran straight into a hillside where it remains to this very day – a rift of finest ochre, as red as gushing blood.

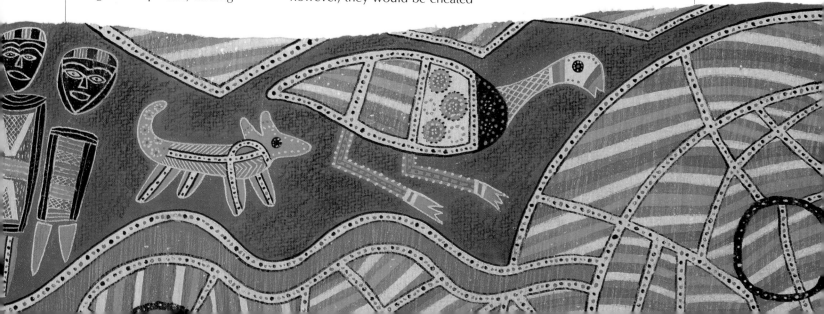

Conceiving Clans and Cultures

A cult of northeastern Arnhem Land celebrates one of the strangest creation myths of all. The travels and exploits of Djanggawul and his two sisters explain the different roles entrusted to men and women.

Just over the horizon from the Arnhem Land coast lay Bralgu, the Isle of the Eternal Beings. Here lived the Djanggawul clan, in love and harmony: one brother and his two sisters-cum-wives. Back in the days of the Dreamtime no laws or customs had been established, so incest could break no taboo. There were no marriages, no moieties, indeed no rules at all to govern the practices of this first of all families. But if their sexual conduct may seem strange by later human standards, their sexual organs were quite extraordinary, trailing on the ground as they walked around. Indeed, the stories claimed that it was to counteract the inconveniences caused by these oversized appendages that the practice of circumcision was introduced.

Despite the difficulties, however, Djanggawul and his older sister Bildjiwuraroiju produced many children together. Miralaidj, much younger, had only just passed puberty, but she too was now lying with her elder brother.

The siblings had come to the island together from another country far across the Arafura Sea, travelling in a bark canoe laden down with different totems and sacred emblems. Bralgu was to be the bridgehead for their landing in Australia: their stay was never intended to be a long one. On reaching this offshore island they devised dances and initiated rituals which they planned to take with them to the nearby continent. Their preparations made ready, they put to sea again for the

The mouth of the Johnston River near Melville Island, along the coast from Arnhem Bay. The region's waterways were conjured into being during the travels of Djanggawul and his sisters.

final leg of their journey, paddling across the rocking waves to the Arnhem Land coastline. They made landfall at Jelangbara, dragging their canoe safely up the beach to a spot which is still sacred to Djanggawul. Here he suggested performing the act of circumcision, but Bildjiwuraroiju disagreed: they should wait until they had reached Arnhem Bay, she said. So, leaving their canoe, they walked along the coast, their organs still trailing on the ground, leaving traces which are still discernible today. When they came to Wabilinga Island they found a population of Baijini people already there, and demanded that they move aside to make way for their own descendants. The Baijini had no choice but to do as they were bidden, but from the ashes of their fires the first charcoal pigment would be made. Djanggawul and his sisters moved on and all down this part of the coast they planted emblems in the earth, conjuring into being a new landscape, establishing the woods, rocks and streams we see today. When they started to strike inland, Djanggawul asked Bildjiwuraroiju to lie with him again: not content with creating this country, he told her, they must people it.

So, settling down here for a time, the brother began breeding upon both sisters; soon both women were producing babies in what seemed a near-continuous stream. The boys they placed in the whiskery grass – they would grow beards when they were older; the girls were sheltered under a mat out of the sun so their skin would remain soft and smooth. Making their way along the coast of Arnhem Bay, they left children and sacred symbols wherever they went. Thus they created, not only the different regions, but the tribes whose descendants would people the hitherto empty Earth, equipping each with its distinct emblems and traditions. But disaster struck one day when the two sisters went out collecting shells and left their hide dilly bags in the shade of a tree. A group of men came creeping up – men who had of course sprung originally from their own female loins. Snatching up the bags, they made off into the bush. Alerted to the theft by a mangrove bird, Bildjiwuraroiju and Miralaidj came running back,

A spirit figure – perhaps modelled on Djanggawul – prances in an ancient rock painting produced in ochres.

to find their sacred symbols all stolen. They could hear the sound of triumphant singing as the men celebrated the theft: the sisters dared not approach their camp, fearful not of the men, but of the powerful magic which was now in male keeping.

Ever since that day it has remained thus, the male elders maintaining mastery over all the most mystical knowledge, eternal keepers of what once was entrusted to the care of women. Their wombs the receptacles of life, their dilly bags the fount of culture, women till then had been the carriers of the Aboriginal future. Now the sisters had to resign themselves to a different role: in future they would spend their time gathering foods from the bush and shore, leaving the more arcane mysteries of existence to the menfolk; but, more importantly, they would be bearers of all lives to come.

45

The Powers of Sibling Pairs

One of the best-known story cycles of all concerns the adventures of two brave and resourceful brothers, Yuree and Wanjel. Often known as the Bram-Bram-Bult, they are among the most familiar figures in Aboriginal myth.

No cloud marked the azure sky or the grazing mammals would have thought the sound was that of distant thunder. No more than a murmuring at first, it grew louder with every second that passed; closer and closer it came, the earth trembling in time with its drumming crescendo. As the quiet creatures looked up in consternation, too terrified to break and flee for their lives, they heard a furious crashing in the undergrowth as saplings were snapped by a seemingly unstoppable force. Suddenly, snorting stertorously in his exertions, streaming sweat as he bounded desperately along, the kangaroo Purra came bursting through the bushes and scudded into the clearing, his body at

breaking-point and his face a mask of anguished terror. His pursuer? A meek-looking glider-possum, who floated effortlessly along in his wake. Doan was his name and, despite his unthreatening appearance, he was a formidable spirit – fit object for Purra's fear. Yet the kangaroo's deepest dread was not to be realized, as it happened, for just as the glider-possum was about to pounce he was attacked in his turn by Wembulin, an echidna, or anteater, camped in the clearing with his two beautiful daughters. Like the possum, the anteater concealed a savage spirit beneath a timorous exterior: within moments he had caught Doan and gobbled him up hungrily. He and his daughters then set off in pursuit of the fleeing Purra.

But these hunters were by now themselves hunted: Doan's maternal uncles, the brothers Yuree and Wanjel, were on their trail. Wondering where their beloved nephew was the brothers had set out to find him, tracking his movements across the Dreamtime landscape. No sign of him could they locate, until they finally saw an ant carrying one of his hairs back to her nest. This aroused their misgivings – suspicions which were reinforced soon after when they saw other ants hauling flakes of his skin and scraps of his bleeding flesh. Weeping, they followed the ants back to the place where what

A bark art image of the kangaroo, a species unique to Australia and a figure in many Aboriginal myths and Dreamtime stories, including the adventure cycle of the Bram-Bram-Bult featuring Purra.

remained of their nephew lay in the undergrowth, now little more than a skeleton. The brush was trampled for several metres around, and a number of trees had been snapped down in the death-struggle. Bent on revenge, the brothers set off to find Wembulin.

Following the trail of his old campfires, they tracked him down on the third day to a little bark shelter outside which his daughters pounded honeysuckle seeds into flour. Taking Wembulin by surprise, the brothers killed him and carried his two daughters off as wives. As they headed homewards, however, they thought better of the matches they had just made: what on earth were they doing entrusting themselves to a pair of women of such dangerous stock? At any moment they might turn on the brothers just as their father had turned on their nephew. They killed their prospective brides, therefore, lest they themselves be betrayed and murdered in their turn.

The Bram-Bram-Bult went on with their adventurous wanderings, roaming far and wide across the land, naming animals, trees, rocks and springs and organizing into living landscape what had previously been blank waste. In time, though, their work neared completion as the Dreamtime approached its close. Tragedy overtook the two brothers, bringing to an end their creative time on Earth. One day, as he fought the venomous serpent Gertuk, the younger brother, Wanjel, was bitten and died. Though Yuree did all he could to save him, he could not restore his brother to life. So, fashioning a replica of his beloved brother from a tree trunk, he ordered it to walk and talk – indeed to take on Wanjel's life where it had left off. In this strange manner reunited, the two brothers continued on their journey westwards, until they finally reached the very end of the Earth, where they lived together in a cave for a long time. Finally, however, they rose into the heavens, whence they look down still, two twinkling, silver stars. Brothers on Earth, they remain together in their heavenly home as that close pair Western astronomers named after the old Roman twins, Castor and Pollux.

The Iguana-men

Sibling pairs played a great part in opening up Aboriginal Australia: Kurukadi and Mumba, the iguana-men, are merely one example of a common mythic type.

These brothers travelled southeastwards from the Kimberley region, naming plants and creatures and fashioning the landscape through much of the western deserts. They hurled their magic boomerang as they went: as it soared back and forth across the desert waste, the land took on form and definition beneath its flight. The iguana-men's journey is thought not to have ended until they had crossed the continent, their travels having taken them across the lands of many peoples. As so often happens in Aboriginal culture, each tribe knows its own section of the "song line" and remains more or less in ignorance of the rest. To the outside observer it is clear, however, that the myth of the iguana-men is one of those tales which spans all Australia, and brings its various, very different peoples together in an unwitting cultural union.

THE BATTLE OF ULURU

The immense, mountain-sized rock called Uluru, some 400 metres in height and with an enormously broad base, occupies a prominent place in the central Australian landscape. Visible from far away Uluru, or Ayers Rock, dominates the surrounding territory and is the most sacred site of many Aboriginal peoples. At this holy place, potent crossing point of countless dreaming tracks and song lines, legends say that two snake peoples once fought for supremacy during the Dreamtime and the rock itself still bears witness to their epic struggle.

Constantly changing in the light, magical Uluru seems to heave with kaleidoscopic life. It is not hard to imagine it as the hub of a continent-wide network of dreaming lines and comes as no surprise to learn it is full of *djang*; nor, come to that, is it difficult to visualize the place as it mythically started – a mass of serpents fighting in the sand.

The Kuniya, or rock-python people, once lived in the desert alongside the Woma, their serpent friends and allies. The Kuniya, however, were restless and questing souls, ever anxious to venture further afield. Their forays took them in the direction of Uluru, although it did not then exist as we know it today, being just another part of the desert's open plain. The Kuniya found it fruitful and liked it so much that they decided to build a new life there. Holding a farewell feast with the Woma, they vowed their enduring loyalty and friendship before striking off for their new home. There they lived contentedly, enjoying the bounty of this rich land – but their idyll was not destined to last long. One day a tribe of venomous Liru –

the deadly carpet-snake – suddenly swept down on the Kuniya camp. A desperate battle began which raged for many hours, and during the seismic upheavals of the conflict, the great rock was born. Marks on its surfaces are said to have been left by weapons or fallen combatants.

Some time after, the Woma decided to pay their old friends a visit. Yet drawing near, and seeing the fate that had befallen their former neighbours, they were quite overcome with grief: they took on snake form, never to return as men.

Born in massacre and shaped in scars, Uluru's appearance marked the end of the creative Dreamtime. At this epoch-making moment the world's creation ceased: from then on the world would be as it was, for better or worse.

Right: Uluru is in the custodianship of the Arrente people. This guide is relating the story of the battle between the Liru and Kuniya, his marks in the sand reminiscent of snake tracks.

Left and above: When the sun starts sinking in the sky the rock transforms as the light works on its hues and colouration, giving the observer an inkling of why this is the most sacred site in the Aborigine's world. The aerial view (above) reveals the immensity of Uluru's base. Visible on the horizon is Katatjuta, a sacred place for female Aborigines that is forbidden to men.

Right: These markings on Uluru's eastern face are considered to be a Kuniya woman's features. The rock was divided into two halves by the Aborigines, reflecting pre-existing territorial boundaries. The sunny side was allocated to the Mala or hare-wallaby people, who preferred the light, the other to the Kuniya people who liked the shade. The Kuniya remain associated with the mythology of the shady side, or Wumbuluru, partly through having buried their eggs at the eastern end of the rock.

Below: The distinctive markings called Ngoru, or The Brain, on the western face reflect the jagged head wounds of an injured warrior. Pockmarks near here are said to have been left by the combatants' spears; while two dark streams (see opposite) are reputed to be fallen Liru. Boulders clustered around the rock's base are often identified with those combatants who fell lifelessly to the ground and were turned to stone.

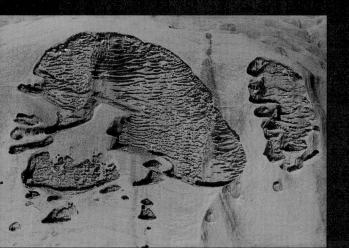

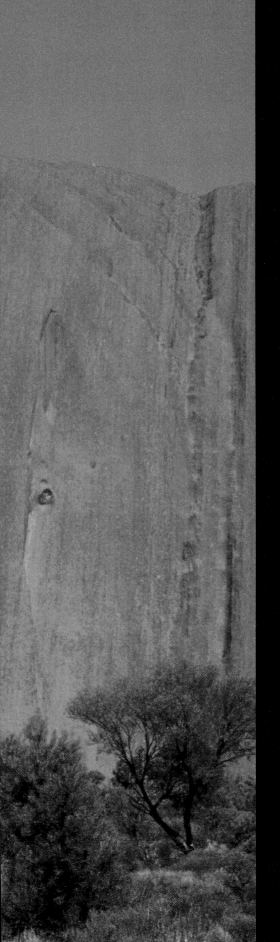

Right: The full knowledge about sacred places and songs is secret and known only to initiates who safeguard it and pass it on solely to those who will respect it on behalf of the people. Elders such as this Arrente man are guardians not only of Uluru but also of their people's rich oral culture.

Below: Rain cascading down the surface of the southwestern face of the rock partially disguises the black-stained watercourses that represent the transformed bodies of two Liru warriors. Above, on top of the rock in Mutijilda gorge, are three rock-holes where Ungata, the Kuniya warriors' leader, died. When the rainwater from these flows down the slopes into the Wanambi pool, it is said to be the transubstantiated blood of the dying Ungata.

THE RICH CYCLE OF LIFE

The Aboriginal people's relationship with nature was symbiotic, and, naturally, this shaped their view of the universe. In their world-view, everything – life forms, landscape, past and present – was inter-related and fluid. Their ancestral spirit beings were human, part-human, or had the ability to change from human to animal or vice versa. These beings gave the Aboriginal people the sto-ries, law and social structure that are still kept alive today through song, ceremony and art. In addition, they merged effortlessly with the environment and its landmarks – thought of as the results of their activities and direct evidence that the stories of the sacred past are true and still exist in the present.

Naradan the bat-man was just such a spirit being. One day in the Dreamtime he found a hive of honey in a hollow tree. He sent one of his wives up the trunk with a stone axe to cut it out, but as she groped about, she slipped and fell. Left hanging by an arm, she screamed out in pain – but it was the thought of losing the honey which afflicted her impatient husband. Naradan severed her arm, whereupon she fell to the ground and bled to death. He then told his other wife to climb up, remove the arm and retrieve the honey. She baulked at such a grisly task, but complied when threatened. Yet she too ended up stuck, and a furious Naradan had to climb up and strike off her arm also. The bat-man found him-self with neither honey nor wives. He slunk homewards shamefully. His eva-sive answers to relatives' questions aroused comment: soon a search-party had found the mutilated wives and it was easy enough to work out what had happened. The people made a fire to burn the murderer, but saw a vague form flitting up into the night. Naradan, now a bat, would from that time on shun the day, hoping to hide his terrible shame under the cloak of darkness.

The myth of Naradan's long-ago crime and punishment is both a stern moral fable and an ingenious account of how things come to be as they are – and more. No mere fairytales, Aboriginal stories are an encyclopaedic record of all Australia's original inhabitants have thought and felt over thou-sands of years. From the origins of species to the elemental structure of the universe, and from the institutions of society to the behaviour of animals and birds: every aspect of life – and of death – finds its commentary in them. To read these stories is to step into another world, ancient and astonishing.

Above: An incised baobab nut from the Kimberley region. A group of Aboriginal men are shown singing and dancing, using clapping sticks and a didjeridoo. The large serpent encircling them symbolizes the inter-relatedness of ceremonies and the natural world.

Opposite: A bark painting from the Northern Territory depicts goannas drinking from a pool. A Dreamtime story tells of a battle between the land and sea animals which ended with the goanna suffering mortal wounds and turning into Mount Maroon.

53

The Unity of People and Nature

The Aborigines expressed their closeness to nature by associating themselves with particular aspects of it, fundamentally influencing their outlook on the world. This totemism meant they traced their ancestry in the natural things about them: in animals, birds and insects – even the rushing wind.

Many inland Aborigines recall the arrival of their ancestors from overseas – the Djanggawul and his sisters, for example, or the Wawilak women who emerged from the waves – but on Groote Eylandt in the windswept waters of the Gulf of Carpentaria, the people look out daily on the sea from which their forbears first stepped. They paddle their canoes to trade and to fish on the very waters from which their ancestors emerged. The islanders cannot help feeling conflicting pulls, to the continent and to the sea from which they came. Marked out by its distinctly Asiatic monsoon climate, the gulf has the feel of a threshold – whose door remains very much ajar. This ambivalence is only underlined, meanwhile, by the gulf's curious meteorological character and the two opposing winds – Bara and Mamariga – whose alternation measures out the northern year.

The Children of the Wind

Every November when Bara begins to stir, the dry air quickens and grows heavy with moisture. Grey clouds dull the tropic sunshine; the atmosphere seems sluggish, yet tense with expectation. The suspense is not long, for the showers themselves follow quickly: soon these northern regions are being battered by rainstorm after rainstorm. Much as it has needed this inundation, nature seems to buckle before its onslaught: the grass is flattened by its force, and trees bow down as if in surrender. Between each fresh dousing, however, the sun shines down on an explosion of fertility as fresh shoots thrust upwards and new buds burgeon on the dripping trees. Water is everywhere and the landscape glints and twinkles like a tilted mirror.

Through December and January the wind blows on, and nature is extravagant in her bounty. Herbs and cereals grow apace, while the trees offer fruit; amid such plenty, the animals and people find life easy and abundant. By February, however, Bara is already faltering, and in April it is usurped by its rival, Mamariga, blowing from the southeast. An altogether different wind, nature seems to crumple before its hot unforgiving blast as on through the dry days of May, June and July it scours away every trace of fresh green from the scene, leaving a landscape of brittle aridity.

Groote Eylandt's Aborigines see it as a warlike invasion. Their tradition holds that Mamariga has seized Bara and imprisoned it in a giant hollow tree on a headland above the sea. Every year, therefore, as November nears, they assemble before the place of captivity, sing sacred incantations and exhortations, and use their axes to strike deep cuts in the bark. Through these apertures, they believe, the wet wind may once more be released into a welcoming world. They encourage it with rites and offerings, bidding it busy itself on their behalf about restoring the rain. So indeed it inevitably turns out: the damp wind blows and the stormclouds gather; within days the first downpour has come to water the gasping earth. Once more all nature bursts forth in fecundity, all living things have the chance to regenerate – until April, when Mamariga will return to abduct its enemy again.

Tribal Moieties

Some Aboriginal peoples honour totem animals (see box, page 57) while others invest physical features of the landscape with sacred energy, but

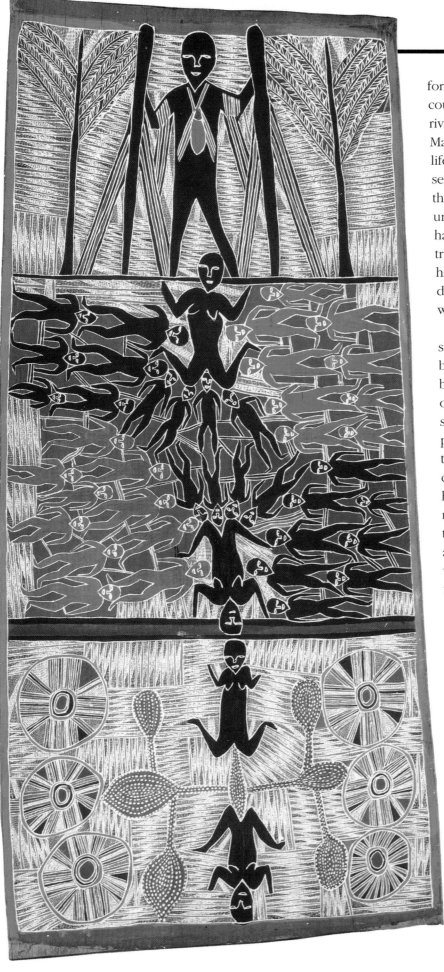

for the people of Groote Eylandt no force could be more powerful than these two rival winds. The opposition of Bara and Mamariga rules all the rhythms of island life, and the cycle of their alternation seems fundamental to the world-view of the people who live there. It is only natural, therefore, that the winds should have come to form the nuclei for their tribal moieties, the complementary halves into which every community is divided and within which men and women must never marry.

The winds which do so much to shape island life are even believed to bring the inhabitants' children, those born into each moiety being blown in on their respective winds. Sailing as spirits down the gusting airways, they put down in the long grass and lurk there until a likely looking woman chances along. Quickly slipping into her body, they settle down in comfort, ready to sit out the long months before their birth in human form. Frank and affirmative as it is about men and women's sexual functions, Aboriginal tradition has tended not to associate sex with reproduction of children. Sexual stimulation from the male may encourage the child growing in the womb, but is not its cause. Rather, human spirits floating free in the air around are "dreamed" into the womb by the mother-to-be, influenced in her turn by watching ancestors.

This painting on eucalyptus bark is a version of the Djanggawul story that is concerned with moieties. The brother stands at the top with his digging-sticks, while below the two sisters give birth to the clans. In the centre this event is shown schematically, while at the bottom it is rendered symbolically.

A Living Water Source

No cycle is more central to Aboriginal existence than the unaccountable alternation of rain and drought, a mysterious rhythm that the frog has come to symbolize. Water cannot simply be awaited; it is vital to have the ability to find it, however arid the landscape.

The Pinnacles Desert might appear a harsh, arid environment – but for those who know where to look, water can be found.

Hunting game or finding honey are important skills but they pale into insignificance beside the art of locating water. Even in more hospitable areas of the Australian interior, long periods may pass between showers, but many Aborigines inhabit deserts in which, from one year's end to the next, untrained eyes would see no trace of water whatsoever. This is no more than an illusion, however, and no Aborigines would be deceived: where an outsider sees dead monotony, they see variety and richness. There may be no surface streams or waterholes, but the water, while not abundant, is there for whoever has the experience and skill to be able to find it. Dig down into the dry sand in any of many long-standing "soaks", for example, and liquid can be found seeping up from the water table. Water is stored too in the fleshy leaves and bulbous roots of particular plants; some grubs and insects are eaten as much for the water as for the food they contain. With many generations of folk memory and experience to draw upon, the Aborigine knows the desert in detail and can find water in dozens of improbable places.

Tiddalik's Torrent

Most valued of all as a living water source is a certain kind of frog found in the desert. Lying deep in the ground, out of reach of the dehydrating sun, it emerges from the earth when it hears the first raindrops falling. It then drinks itself into a bloated stupor before going to ground once more as it feels the atmosphere drying. Invaluable as its sponge-like body may be to Aborigines as a source of water, its significance as a symbol is greater still. Soaking up moisture as the arid earth does the soft rain, its strange life seems analogous to the desert cycle of deluge and drought.

With their amphibious ways and their glistening skins, frogs are generally associated with water. Typical was Tiddalik, the biggest frog that ever existed. Waking one morning with a powerful thirst he drank – and did not stop drinking till he had drunk the whole world dry. All creation was soon shrivelling up around him. As first the plants and then the trees started to die, the animals knew that they could not be far behind. So, meeting in council, they attempted to form a plan to get Tiddalik to release water. One scheme after another was raised and rejected – none seemed at all likely to work, until a wise old wombat came up with a plan all agreed stood a chance of succeeding. If the giant frog could be made to laugh, said the sage, the water would come pouring forth in a torrent from his mouth: their problems would at last be at an end.

In practice, though, making Tiddalik laugh proved no easy matter. The kookaburra's best jokes fell flat and died. The kangaroo and emu leaped about in farce, the lizard strutted comically, but Tiddalik sat stony-faced. Just as they were all despairing, however, the animals were joined by Nabunum the eel, only now driven from his home in the creek by the retreating water. He danced on his sinuous tail, assuming all manner of improbable positions, until at last the frog could no longer help himself but roared with laughter. The torrent gushed forth just as the wise old wombat had predicted: the land was watered, lakes, rivers and billabongs were all refilled.

Animal Totems

Totemism – the use of life forms as patron spirits – was central in the Aboriginal world. It underlined the close bond between man and nature, influenced social groupings, inspired stories and rituals, and connected people to the mythic past.

No sentimentality dictates the sympathy and understanding on which the ancient Aboriginal lifestyle was founded: it has been vital to human survival in a fragile environment. Compelled by tradition to respect his own and his neighbours' totems, the Aborigine can never see himself as an exploiting lord of nature, rather as a careful steward: for he is merely one part of a wider scheme.

Totemism classified all living things and natural phenomena in a single system, but to work it had to function on numerous levels. It began with the individual, escalating through gender, moiety, tribe, region, and so on. Thus the totem was the manifestation of a relationship with the entire world, linking Aborigine and totem in a mutual bond, celebrated through song, ritual and story.

One important role was as a barrier to in-breeding, the two separate moieties of the typical tribe being subdivided into up to eight totemic classes. The Matthurie moiety of the southern Australian Urbanna people, for example, comprised separate duck and dingo, cicada, emu, wild turkey and black swan sections. The opposing, Kirarawa moiety contained a further six totemic groups: the cloud and carpet snake, the lace lizard and pelican, the waterhen and crow.

Djirrban, an ancestral figure whose body is covered with the designs he distributed to the Yirritja moiety clans of Arnhem Land.

57

The Greatest Gift

With its life-giving light and warmth, fire is often regarded in Aboriginal society as a feminine element, although its release for the benefit of humanity was the work of men. Fire's genesis, however, is mysterious. Mythic theories abound as to how the gift of fire was first gained, but certain common themes – either man-made or naturally occurring – recur.

Birds of the Sacred Flame

The feminine link with fire explains the story told in Victoria of how the wise women were duped out of their flame by the trickster crow-man. This theft of fire from its female custodians characteristically earns punishment, as when the crow-man burns himself black (see pages 60–61). In parts of Arnhem Land the women's fire was stolen by their sons, who were then turned into crocodiles.

A Queensland version of the tale describes how the wren got his red tail feathers. Resolved that no one else should share his precious possession, he tucked a burning coal away beneath his tail. Too late he registered the acrid smell as his rump began to singe: ever since he has had red tail feathers in token of his selfish deed.

For other story-tellers it was Mar, the cockatoo-man, who wanted to keep fire's secret to him-

self: the other Aborigines sent the little bird-man, Takkanna, to spy on Mar to see what he could find out. Peering out from the undergrowth one day as Mar prepared to cook meat, Takkanna watched as the cockatoo-man made a little pile of dry grass and bark kindling. He looked on as Mar reached under the feather headdress he always wore. From it he picked a burning coal, which he used to light his fire before returning it to its hiding place.

Waiting till Mar's attention was elsewhere, Takkanna reached out with a little stick, which he held in the fire until it was well alight. Then he ran off quietly through the bush, hoping to be back at his camp before Mar noticed. Unfortunately, however, sparks spilled from the brand and caused a huge conflagration in the dry grassland. Mar could hardly fail to see a blaze which was threatening to engulf the whole country: with a yell of rage he stopped his cooking and gave chase. A huge battle then ensued between Mar and Takkanna's comrades. As they fought in mounting frenzy, all the participants were turned into birds: Mar flew off screaming, transformed into a cockatoo. Where once he had worn a headdress, now he wore a feathered crest, marked a rich red where he had concealed his precious fire. Takkanna, for his part, was turned into a friendly rosella, his warm red breast an enduring reminder of the heroic selflessness with which he had sought fire for all.

Heavenly Firesticks

Along Australia's northwest coast a different tale is told: there fire is thought to have been brought down to Earth from the heavens. No lightning-bolt brought it down, but two brothers, Kanbi and Jitabidi, who hitherto had always lived in the star-strewn sky. They dwelled near the Southern Cross, whose four "pointers" were thought to be their fires, but once they were forced to descend to Earth for a time by a famine in their own airy hunting grounds. Bringing their firesticks with them so as to be able to cook anything that they caught, they came down, set up camp and went off hunting opossums. They were gone so many hours that their firesticks grew bored and restless. Finally, forgetting their duty, they got up and began playing about, chasing one another through the grass and scrambling in and out of trees. So boisterous was their game that the resulting friction caused a fire, and soon the whole countryside was aflame. From a distance, Kanbi and Jitabidi saw the trouble and made straight back to camp, where they rounded up their firesticks and returned heavenwards.

Behind them they left the world's first-ever fire burning. When a party of Aborigines came upon it they could not believe their eyes. Seeing its light and feeling its warmth, they immediately sensed the value of their find. Taking burning brands to start their own fires, they nurtured the gift. All subsequent fires having been descended from that one, all share the same heavenly ancestry in the Southern Cross.

Loved and feared in just about equal measures in the Aboriginal order, fire is simultaneously the cosy focus of domestic existence and a force for fearful environmental destruction. Reflected in the story of Mar and Takkanna, Australia's fierce bush fires are legendary. The Aboriginal people, however, tried to harness fire, using it as an aid to hunting – to drive game from an impenetrable thicket – and a means of regenerating bush vegetation through the creation of fertile, nourishing ashes.

The Embodiment of the Eaglehawk

Much more than a rivalry between mere birds – the one the symbol of imperious grace and strength, the other the wily scavenger – the conflict of the eaglehawk and the crow embodies some of the Aborigines' strictest conventions and deepest taboos.

Stories abound of the conflict between the eaglehawk and the crow, and all tend to end in stalemate. While the crow can never hope to conquer the noble strength of the soaring eaglehawk, nor can the eaglehawk match the crow's cunning. The obstinate opposition between the two birds has made their relationship a symbol of oil-and-water incompatibility, hence its widespread use in Aboriginal societies for marking out the moieties. Although evident in every aspect of their ritual and art, the fundamental purpose of these dualities is the reinforcement of the incest taboo. Incest – with all its degenerative implications for the gene-pool – is a more present and potent danger in a small and isolated hunter-gatherer group than in a modern city. The moiety system helps attain this end, by reinforcing the universal taboo. Alliances within the moieties are strictly forbidden: crow must marry eaglehawk, and eaglehawk wed crow.

Mulyan the Eaglehawk-man

The eaglehawk-crow rivalry has its origins deep in the Dreamtime when the two birds were created. In Murray River country, the Aborigines explain the enmity this way: Mulyan the eaglehawk-man, say the story-tellers, once married a lovely girl from the crow community. They lived happily together, and she bore him a fine son. One day, however, he became convinced that he had seen her flirting with a magpie-man: in his rage he beat her so savagely that she died. Learning of his sister's treatment, her brother, Wahn the crow-man, was filled with anger, and started scheming his revenge. But given the eaglehawk's power, he knew he would have to proceed by strategy rather than strength: in any case, revenge, he felt, was a dish best eaten cold. He waited, therefore, until his nephew had grown to adolescence, before turning up – apparently tired and weary – at Mulyan's camp. The eaglehawk-man showed him every hospitality, then set out hunting: no sooner had he left than the crow murdered Mulyan's beloved son. Running about the camp, trampling down the grass and bushes, he attempted to make the place look like the scene of a mass-ambush and ensuing battle. When his host returned that evening, this was the story Wahn duly told: a band of intruders had attacked the camp, he said, and despite all his own best endeavours, they had killed the boy before melting away again into the bush.

Grief warred in Mulyan's heart with anger, for he could clearly see that his guest was lying: all the tracks round the campfire were plainly his. But Mulyan too was capable of strategy: instead of accusing the killer there and then, he sadly asked him to help him dig a grave for his child. All sympathy and support, the crow-man willingly agreed.

He started digging deeper and deeper. When he was several feet down, his head well below ground-level, Mulyan suddenly started shovelling the earth back, burying the murderer alive. He filled the grave right in and tamped the soft soil down till it was quite hard: the crow-man would assuredly be dead now, he thought. Yet he was wrong: Wahn's magic saved him. He summoned up a thunderstorm to cover his escape, during which a lightning-bolt ignited Mulyan's camp. Watching the inferno in triumph, however, Wahn saw Mulyan float up and fly away, the eaglehawk-man spared to live on as an actual eaglehawk. The crow did not escape unscathed either, for he was scorched by his own lightning – so badly that his feathers were charred black from that day on.

The Blackening of the Crow

Only seven wise women originally understood the mystery of fire, say the Aboriginal people of Victoria: all through the Dreamtime they guarded their secret jealously. The cunning crow-man was no respecter of other people's property: by hook or by crook, he resolved to find out what they knew.

First ingratiating himself with the sacred guardians by flattery and gifts, he was soon sharing their conversation and assisting them in their work. He was not slow to notice that they carried flames of fire on the tips of their digging-sticks; nor that they loved to eat termites, but were terrified of snakes. So, carefully concealing a knot of coiling serpents in a termites' nest, he went to see his new friends and invited them to join him in a banquet. They followed him eagerly to the termite mound and broke it open with the utmost glee – only to fall back in horror when the snakes spilled forth in a writhing, hissing mass. Laying about them in a panic, the women failed to notice the flames falling from their sticks. The crow-man gathered them up, and nursed the fire in some soft bark kindling. Now it was he who hugged the secret to himself, refusing to share it with anyone. Beset by constant questions from men anxious to acquire fire for themselves, his selfishness was almost his undoing. Losing his temper with one man who seemed unprepared to take no for an answer, he hurled a burning coal at him, but the missile fell short and set fire to the very patch of ground on which the crow himself was sitting. It seemed to those who saw the resulting blaze that he must surely be burned to a crisp – till suddenly they saw his blackened body stir in the smoke and flame and take wing to a nearby tree. From there he cawed at them mockingly, the sooty-feathered crow that he has remained ever since.

The Diversity of Birds

Australia's native bird life is astonishing in its variety, and so too is the rich Aboriginal mythology to which it has given rise. A wealth of stories set out to explain how the vast array of bird species has become so different in looks and lifestyle.

Sometimes birds appear straightforwardly as the establishing ancestors of a people: Naarait the white cockatoo, for example, who ordained the rules for the gatherings of the Rimberunga people of southeast Arnhem Land. From the exact colour and pattern of their body-paint to the musical instruments they should play and the rhythms they should beat, the bird laid down the procedures to the last detail. The story is valued for its sacred status, a key component in the tribe's living heritage.

The Night Herons and the Reeds

Many myths serve simultaneously as entertainment and "just so stories", accounting for some aspect or other of the creation amid which the story-tellers lived. The New South Wales tale of the night herons and the reeds is a perfect example. A particular tribe there, it is said, was so bullied by stronger neighbours that it finally sought refuge in a change of shape. Tired of life as put-upon humans, the tribespeople turned themselves into a flock of herons and encamped in a swamp.

Despite being remote from the attentions of their old persecutors, they none the less continued to feel anxious and exposed. Their former life had made them jittery, and the swamp afforded little in the way of real cover. Reeds in those days were little more than straggly stalks of glorified grass, nothing like high enough to conceal a tall heron. And so, huddling each night behind the stunted clumps, they pulled at the tops, trying to stretch them higher in the hope of finding some real concealment from their imagined enemies.

Over time the reeds were extended to their present length – tall enough to hide a heron – but nothing would allay fears which were by now habitual. Despite the impenetrability of the reeds, the herons still shun the daylight hours, emerging to hunt only in the dark of the night. If you examine the reed stems carefully, meanwhile, you can see the raised bump where the herons once grasped them, stretching them with all their strength that they might grow taller.

An emu depicted on rock in white ochre. One myth recounts that the emu was originally a heavenly sky-bird who visited Earth and was tricked into cutting off her wings. The kookaburra laughed to see it and still does so every time he remembers.

How Swans Became Black

A story from the fertile region of the east Australian seaboard sees the old trickster crow entering an unlikely alliance with the elegant swan which falls foul of the crow's traditional enemy, the eagle-hawk. Two white swans (for in the Dreamtime all Australia's swans were white) enraged the eagle-hawks when they unwittingly landed on a lagoon which was eaglehawk territory. The eaglehawk forces swooped down and attacked them ruth-lessly, tearing at them with their talons and their hooked beaks, pulling out great tufts of down and feathers as they bore them southwards along the coast. The dazzling white plumes floated gently to earth where they turned into beautiful flowers: the flannel flowers which each spring bedeck the east Australian coastal clifftops. The eaglehawks finally dropped the swans' bodies, practically plucked bare, in a desert spot, then, leaving their defeated enemy for dead, they headed homewards. A flock of crows happened by, and seeing the swans where they lay broken-spirited and chilled, felt sympathy with a fellow enemy of the cruel eagle-hawk. Since the swans had no feathers left, they plucked out plumage of their own for them to wear – and Australian swans were black as crows from that day forward.

Rival Sisters Emu and Turkey

It is a long way from the grandeur of the eagle-hawk and the poise of the gliding swan to the comical gait of the emu and the wild turkey. Yet they too had their hour in an ungainly war which has marked out the different species in perpetuity.

The story takes place at a time when food was short and strongly competed for, and starts when the two birds – then sisters – were locked in a silly sibling rivalry, in which Kalaia the emu envied Kipara the turkey for the privileges she appeared to enjoy as her elder. The slow-witted emu managed to conjure up what was actually quite a cunning ruse, hiding all but two of her chicks in long grass well away from her nest. When her sister asked where the others were,

A wooden figure of a black *gadaga* bird, an animal associated with Muruwiri Rocks where turtle-man's spirit resides, in the Arnhem Land territory of the Dua moiety. The bird is perched on timber as if it were drifting in the sea.

Kalaia replied with the utmost aplomb that she had killed all but two to stretch out the available food. Loving mother that she was, the turkey was shocked by such a harsh scheme, but she had to admit she could find no flaw in its logic. So, taking her chicks off into the Outback, she like-wise did all but two to death, only to find on returning home that Kalaia's family was intact and she had been cheated.

Dull as she was, however, Kipara was not without wiles of her own, and she vowed to be revenged on her spiteful sister. Folding her wings back upon themselves, she told Kalaia she had cut them off halfway. She felt a new bird, she said leaping and dancing, so light and so physically free she could not think why she had not done it years before. Not to be outdone, Kalaia seized a stone knife and started hacking at her own wings: soon only short, useless stumps remained. At that Kipara spread her own pinions wide and cried out in triumph: Kalaia would never again be able to fly and she might be hunted down with ease by dogs and men. At least she would have her chicks, Kalaia retorted, seeing how she had been tricked, whereas Kipara had lost all but two of hers. And so it would turn out: from that time forwards the emu would be flightless, while the turkey would never hatch more than two chicks at a time.

A Story-Filled Landscape

For the Aborigines, the basic elements of existence – earth and water as much as animals, plants and people – were regarded as having powerful animating spirits of their own. Earth was always more than inert rock and sand; and water was never merely a characterless fluid.

The strange, steep-sided circular lakes clustered around Mount Gambier have a colourful explanation among the district's Aboriginal tribes. They are the work of the giant Craitbul and his sons, who once dwelled not far away near Mount Muirhead. They lived in abject poverty, scratching a sparse living from unyielding soil. They possessed only one tool between them, a wooden digging-stick: apart from this they had only their bare hands with

which to scrabble for roots and tubers in the stony earth. It was a hard, though not unhappy, life. One night, however, this austere idyll was brought abruptly to a violent end: an unknown enemy fell on Craitbul's camp, and the giant and his sons fled for their lives. They ended up on Mount Gambier, where they thought they would be safe. And so indeed it turned out – no enemy would ever find them there – yet life still had its tribulations. The first oven they dug in the earth filled up with water from below without any warning. So it turned out with a second and a third: the water came welling up as if from nowhere. When the fourth flooded, Craitbul concluded that destiny did not mean them to stay there. So, taking their digging-stick, they set off in search of a new home.

Flowers of Blood

A tragic love story is told in Australia's central region to account for certain features of the landscape. A young girl, Purlimil, was promised by her people's elders to a jealous, unpleasant old man named Turlta. Purlimil was doubly desolate: not only did she hate the old lecher, but she loved the handsome Borola, and now would have to let him go. The young lovers decided to run away together.

The crater-lakes of Mount Gambier are the result not of ancient volcanic activity but of the Dreamtime work of the giant Craitbul and his sons, according to the tales told by local Aborigines.

"Sturt's Desert Peas", the botanists call them, but the local Aborigines know better. To them they will always be the "Flowers of Blood". Every year, where innocent tribespeople fell, the ground is carpeted anew by a fresh throng of red flowers, each with its coal black centre, like countless eyes transfixing the beholder with a reproachful stare.

Their resolve hardened as the betrothal approached, and eventually, on the night before Purlimil was due to wed, she and her lover stole away into the bush. They wandered until finally a friendly tribe took them in and they settled down to stay in their camp. So happy were the two that within a few years they had almost forgotten the elopement. Old Turlta, however, remembered all too clearly: his bitterness had grown with time.

One day Turlta mustered his male relatives into a large warband and they attacked the camp of Purlimil and Borola's adoptive tribe. They killed everybody in it – their innocent blood stained the desert sand for kilometres around. Turlta felt so fulfilled as a result of this bloodletting, he even came back the year after to see his victims' bones. To his surprise, however, there were none visible. Instead he shuddered to feel the black eyes of a host of blood-red flowers staring up at him accusingly: the souls, he instinctively knew, of those he had slain. Turning to flee a field where the spirits of the dead were clearly very much alive, Turlta had gone only a few steps before he was brought down by a spear which flew out of nowhere.

Spring of the Dingo-men

A spring at Nirgo, in the central desert area, is said to have been dug by two dingo-men, Munbun and Kapiri, who found themselves stranded without water. To increase their chances of success, the two dug in opposite directions: Munbun to the north and Kapiri, the elder, working south. Kapiri it was who found the bountiful source of refreshing water. When two Aboriginal elders happened along, the dog-men invited them to dig their fill, telling them that when they had gone the old men could have it for ever after. Overwhelmed by such generosity, the men founded special laws among their people for the hunting of the dingo. Hunters might still kill the father, they ruled, but the mothers and pups must not henceforth be harmed.

For generations the decree was honoured, but then one man saw fit to ignore it: he killed and cooked a pair of cubs and calmly ate them. Their enraged mother howled in anguish and set out to find the killer and wreak her vengeance. Hearing her cry, the hunter fled in terror of his life, finally taking refuge in the highest tree-top he could find. Helped by her fellow dingoes, the mother dug away at the roots below until finally the tree toppled and came crashing to earth. Its human occupant was killed instantly, but by some miracle the pups he had killed and eaten were brought back to life. The hole in the ground where the tree was uprooted can still be seen, while round about lie red boulders – congealed drops of the blasphemer's spattered blood.

65

Koopoo the First Kangaroo

Aboriginal animal myths enshrine many traditions and taboos. Like their own human ancestors, the first kangaroo is said to have arrived from the north, across the sea. Koopoo was his name, according to the peoples of Arnhem Land for whom he is a founding father.

The Djauan tell the tale of how Koopoo gifted their most sacred rituals, giving their forbears clear instructions as to how they were to celebrate their corroboree: its rites, its rhythms and its songs. He brought with him in a bag of hide the white paint with which they were to decorate their bodies. Keeper of the Djauan's spiritual and social heritage, he protected it from would-be thieves in a number of confrontations.

The Djauan's near neighbours, the Yungmun people, also commemorate Koopoo. They recall how he formed the spring from which the Flying Fox River flows, before being attacked by a dingo that wanted to steal it – the Yungmun's liquid inheritance. His kangaroo kin were scattered by the dog's violence, taking flight in every direction. Where they came to deep rivers they fashioned fords so as to be able to cross; in the dry wastes they created springs and streams. Koopoo headed off to the Waterhouse River in whose shallows he dug out a trench; he transformed himself into a Rainbow Snake and hid in the dark water. From there he would rule as the Yungmun's proprietary spirit, watching over their heritage and identity.

Koopoo's story symbolizes the Aborigines' own: arrival in Australia and adjustment to its environment. To understand the kangaroo's experiences is to understand much about the Aborigines themselves: the landscape and the traditions which have shaped them. But whereas tales such as Koopoo's seem to enshrine a people's whole system of values, others provide more particular insights into aspects of the world in which the first story-tellers lived. One myth not only gives a very different account of the kangaroo's origins, but also explains its avoidance of the wombat – a phenomenon still evident in the natural world today.

The Kangaroo and the Wombat

In the distant days of the Dreamtime, Mirram and Wareen roamed the wilderness together, hunting. Inseparable friends, they shared one another's food and were alike in every taste but one: at night Wareen insisted on a shelter, however rough and ready, but Mirram was happier in the open air. One fateful night, however, it rained so torrentially that Mirram's fire was extinguished. While not normally bothered by rain, this storm was so violent that he decided he must ask his friend to grant him shelter. But Wareen, roused from sleep, was feeling far too cantankerous to have any time for Mirram's problems. Why, he asked irritably, should he make room for someone who had been too lazy to erect cover of his own? Staggered to find such an attitude in a friend for whom he would have given everything he had, Mirram flew into a rage. He seized a large stone and threw it hard at his companion's head: it struck him on the forehead, flattening it completely. Wareen hurled his spear in response: it stuck deep at the base of Mirram's spine and would not be shifted, no matter how hard it was tugged. In time it grew fur and thickened, forming itself into a long tail, while Mirram himself took on the form of the kangaroo. Retaining this shape right down to the present, Mirram still feels the same love for the open plain, preferring its endless expanses to any amount of cover. This lifestyle also has the advantage of keeping him well clear of his old enemy, the flat-faced wombat Wareen, who seldom ventures far from the deep hole in which he lives.

An x-ray style bark painting of a kangaroo with a stick-like Mimi spirit hunter. The x-ray is a respectful way of showing the whole living being of the animal and not just its external form.

Gifts of Swamp and Sea

Like the Australian landscape itself, Aboriginal lifestyles varied widely. People adapted themselves to tropical wetlands as well as the arid, inland deserts, and the mythologies of the coastal and island peoples are rich in stories about all forms of aquatic life.

Many generations ago in the Dreamtime a group of bandicoot-men lived on Australia's tropical northern coast. Despite dwelling by the sea, though, they had no canoes and remained landsmen through and through. Their life ashore was not so harsh – there was plenty of food to be found in the woods and swamps – but they could not help hankering after the abundance of the sea. On top of that a tiny island lay tantalizingly close to the coast, with herds of game and fruit-laden trees on it. Without a canoe, however, this paradise might as well have been at the other end of the Earth.

Getting hold of a canoe, however, was much more easily said than done. The only dugout along the coast was owned by Ulamina, a starfish-man, and he kept this most prized possession to himself. The bandicoot-men begged and pleaded, but the starfish-man remained unmoved, even by favours and gifts. One bandicoot-man, Banguruk, finally decided that enough was enough: he would steal the canoe, whatever the consequences might be. Subtlety was required, so Banguruk redoubled his efforts to charm its owner. Plying the starfish-man with offerings and bombarding him with assistance in this task and that, he succeeded in making himself indispensable to Ulamina.

So it was that the starfish-man asked him one day to accompany him on a turtle-hunt: they would of course have to go out in the canoe. They

Lotus lily pads and palms dotting this lush billabong near the mouth of the Mary River hint at the teeming abundance of plant and animal life forms available to the Aboriginal peoples of the northern regions of Australia.

landed a large turtle which Banguruk carried ashore – then kept on walking. Ulamina followed him unsuspectingly as he bore the turtle some distance across the dunes. By the time he set it down and started a cooking-fire the sea was completely out of sight. In time the starfish-man did begin to wonder why they had not cooked dinner on the shore: he sat up with a start as he thought of his precious canoe. Running back to the crest of the sandhills he looked down to see the bandicoot-men paddling his boat away. He chased after them into the breakers but by that time they were well out to sea: he sank to the bottom in his despair, and was transformed into a starfish. He can still be seen waving his arms in agitation, hoping against hope that he might catch the canoe which was stolen from him so long ago. The bandicoot-men, meanwhile, forsook dry land for a new lifestyle in which they would reap the harvest – and face the hazards – of the sea.

Yambirika and the Isles of Plenty

On the many islets of the Gulf of Carpentaria, life begins and ends with the sea. Birds' eggs and shellfish, seals and porpoises add variety to the local Aborigines' staple diet of fish. So large did the sea loom in the consciousness of the ancient inhabitants of the area's Bickerton Island that they assumed their home floated on the gulf like a raft. They told the story of how the sea became populated with the parrot-fish on which they depend after Yambirika the parrot-fish-man tired of life ashore. He dug a hole right through the island and slipped into the sea, in whose waters his descendants have dwelled ever since. Yambirika himself was turned into a rock, which still protrudes a little way above the waves. The Aborigines visit the site each year to do him honour. By throwing slivers of stone in all directions and chanting incantations to Yambirika, they believe they can increase the stock of parrot-fish in the sea. Not only that, but by their ancestor's influence the parrot-fish can, it is firmly believed, be encouraged to offer themselves easily to the Aborigines' lines.

A rich variety of Arnhem Land swamp creatures, including birds and fish, are shown in this Aboriginal bark painting. This tropical region is home to more than 100 mammal and reptile species and one-third of all Australia's birds, inspiring many of the area's mythological stories.

69

Wonders of the Heavens

Complementing those from the land and the sea, countless more Aboriginal ancestor spirits gaze down from the starry sky. A wondrous show, the Australian heavens shimmer with a lively display of glinting and twinkling from old friends familiar from many tales.

The lone hunter peered into the Outback night trying to orientate himself: he might be anywhere. Far above, in the great vault of the heavens, a throng of starry spirits formed a mass of blazing brilliance. Vast constellations and separate points of light alike, they winked down companionably, reminding him that he need never be alone.

The Southern Cross

At the heart of the night sky are the four stars of the Southern Cross. One tradition among a great many (see page 59) explains that the component stars are the daughters of Mululu, a tribal chief. Fearful as his death approached that he was leaving his girls with no brother to protect them, he asked them to come and join him in the sky. They should go and see a certain medicine-man, he said – they would know him by his long, thick beard – and he would help them make the ascent. Mululu duly died, and his loving daughters set out to honour his instructions. After many days searching they found the man, whose luxuriant beard seemed to go on for ever. He plaited it into a rope, and up it they climbed. Fear gripped the girls, but they kept on going all the way to the sky, where they were reunited with Mululu. Forming a joyous family group, the sisters became the four pointers of the Southern Cross, while Mululu watches over them as the star astronomers call Centaurus.

Spirit of the Moon

Some say the moon is the spirit of Mityan, a native cat who fell in love with and fought for the most beautiful of the wives of Unurginite, of the constellation Canis Major. Driven off in defeat, he has

The Aborigines have a rich astral mythology. The stars and constellations are said to be ancestors who have ascended into the sky and are sitting around their campfires. Many tales associate the moon with the bringing of death into the world.

roamed the skies forlornly ever since, hoping that he may one day be reunited with his lost love.

Another story tells how the moon-man Alinda fell out with the parrot-fish-man Dirima, the two finally fighting so violently that each died of their wounds. Although Alinda ascended into the heavens and Dirima dived into the sea, the two continued with their bickering. Implacable in his hostility, the moon-man ruled that once the parrot-fish died, it might never return to life. All other living things were included in this curse – even Alinda himself, though he managed to contrive a partial reprieve. He only "dies" temporarily before resuming his life-cycle, with the old full moon falling into the sea to become the round nautilus shell.

The Boomerang and the Sun

From the Aborigine people of the Flinders Range of southern Australia comes the astonishing story of how the distinction first arose between night and day – for in the world's infancy, it seems, all was light and sunshine, with no intervening darkness.

The trouble started one Dreamtime day when the goanna lizard and the gecko set out to visit neighbours. On arrival, however, they found that their friends had all been massacred: with one voice they vowed vengeance upon those responsible. It had, it soon transpired, been the sun-woman and her dingo dogs who had attacked and killed the defenceless community: she was a formidable foe, but the goanna and the gecko were quite undaunted. As the sun-woman stormed and shouted her defiance, the lizard drew his boomerang and hurled it – and dashed the sun clean out of the sky. It plummeted over the western horizon, plunging the world into total darkness – and now the lizard and the gecko really were alarmed. What would become of them without the sun-woman and her warming, illuminating rays? They must do everything they could to restore her to the heavens. The goanna took another boomerang and hurled it westwards with all his might to where he had seen his target disappearing. It fell ineffectually to ground so he threw two others to the south and north, but they too drifted back without hitting anything. In despair, the goanna took his last boomerang and launched it into the eastern sky – the opposite direction from that in which he had seen the sun-woman sinking. To his astonishment it returned, driving before it the sun's burning sphere, which tracked westwards across the sky before disappearing. From that day on the sun maintained this course, rising in the east and setting in the west, lighting up the day for work and hunting and casting the night into shade for sleeping. All agreed this was an ideal arrangement, and the Aborigines of the Flinders have felt a debt of gratitude to the goanna and the gecko ever since.

Turning the World Upside-down

Life for Australia's Aborigines has never been easy: nature has always been the most fickle of friends. The bad times have been many, and the best have often been ambushed by disaster, with fire or flood, drought or storm sweeping everything away. A paradoxical part of Aboriginal belief was therefore the disorder introduced by trickster figures.

Both the unpredictability of nature and the malice and perversity of humans are captured in Aboriginal mythology in the figure of the trickster. The deeds of these unruly, disruptive and at times disturbing beings range from the simply high-spirited to the downright evil. But all share an overriding instinct to upset the normal order of things, whether in whimsical pranks or more sinister doings. So determinedly do they work to disrupt the smooth running of the Aboriginal cosmos that some scholars have concluded that they are relics of an earlier world system, adapted – but never fully reconciled – to the new order which was introduced with the cult of ancestral heroes.

Yet, disruptive as he is, does the trickster really represent such a dramatic departure for the ancestral tradition? Any creed which fails to identify and accommodate the problem of evil is surely an inadequate response to the realities of the world. The trickster can thus be seen as being every bit as vital to the cult of the ancestors as the dingo or the Rainbow Snake.

Upsetting Order

The trickster does, admittedly, come across as mean-spirited by comparison. The Ngandjala-Ngandjala

of the western Kimberleys, for example, wander through the bush like tearaways looking for trouble. Blighting a carefully tended food source here, they whisk away a long-standing patch of berries there, to the bemusement of the women when they come to reap the expected harvest.

As with other tricksters, however, their influence is not exclusively evil: they can upset the normal order for better as well as worse. Hence their more appealing trick of cooking plants and fruit to make them ripen before their time. During the monsoon season, clouds of mist may be seen rising from the ground: these, it is said, are the fires on which the Ngandjala-Ngandjala have been preparing an early harvest. Their near neighbours the Wurulu-Wurulu make a nuisance of themselves by stealing honey which the Aborigines would like for themselves: they tie bushy flowers to the end of long stalks and poke them into the hives to extract it. When an Aborigine finds a hive of bees and it turns out to be empty of honey, he knows he has been beaten to it by this exasperating trickster.

Trickster spirits lived in many places, including rock itself. Nourlangie Rock in the Northern Territory is famous for its rock art figures, some executed in bold ochre colours.

Yam-Woman and Arrowroot-Man

A staple for many Aboriginal peoples, the yam inevitably has a special place in their scheme of things. Cultivated and cooked by the women, it tends to be identified with the feminine principle in general and pregnancy in particular, as a story told by the Wik Munggan, of Cape York Peninsula, shows.

In the Dreamtime, before things had taken on their present forms, the yam was a woman herself. Not far from her lived the arrowroot – then a man. The two met and fell in love, living together as man and wife: but their relationship was always quarrelsome, and in the course of time they parted. Before many days had passed, however, the woman started to feel queasy and out of sorts. Pregnant, she scraped out a little hollow in the ground in the hope of making herself more comfortable. She had to dig herself in deeper and deeper to accommodate her bulging figure, but the further down she sank, the more claustrophobic and hot she felt. The sun beat down and she thirsted for water. She was desperate now to escape but the sides were steep and she could not climb them. In time she resigned herself to her imprisonment, recognizing it as a part of her reproductive function: from this hole would issue an abundance of yams for future women to cook for food.

Unpredictable Interferers

Rock paintings on boulders and cave walls are a target for the tricksters' more sinister attentions. In interfering with these icons they can call into question a people's whole cultural continuity. The Ngandjala-Ngandjala, for instance, like to vandalize the paintings of ancestral heroes, obliterating them by painting their own self-portraits on top, asserting their ownership of the site.

Another Kimberley trickster, the Argula, paints grotesque pictures of his intended victims, who then find themselves afflicted by disfigurements, disabilities – even death. Since the Argula often only paints wrong-doers, his influence is, in its way, benign: at least not straightforwardly "evil" in the Judaeo-Christian sense.

The Mimi, whose slender forms can be seen painted on cliff faces all along the Arnhem Land escarpment, has artistic interests too. The area's Aborigines assume the portraits are the work of the trickster spirits themselves since they were done before their own ancestors arrived. The Mimi too are ambiguous, capable of good as well as evil: they are said to have taught humans how to hunt. Their mood is unpredictable, though, especially when their privacy is being invaded: for this reason wayfarers call out warnings to them at intervals when walking through the bush.

Altogether more fearsome is Arnhem Land's Namorodo. Flying fast through the air in the deep of the night, he slashes with long claws at anyone he hears. People listen in dread for the swishing sound that announces his approach, a terrible death at his hands the very least of their worries. For the Namorodo claims not only the victim's body but also his immortal soul: once he has it he recruits it to his own company. Instead of finding happy peace with its totemic ancestors, the dead soul will itself have to wander the night, another Namorodo on the prowl for human flesh.

Mysteries of the Spirit World

The Aborigines shared their territories with a host of assorted spirits. Most were harmless but some posed a grave threat to human life. Spirits lay in the forests, among the hills and under the water, but they might also pass as human and live among the people themselves.

A spirit of Arnhem Land's tropical forest, the reclusive Garkain lived on a diet of human flesh and blood. Sneaking up behind any intruder – or flying swiftly through the air – he would envelop the trespasser in a flurry of arms and legs. Flaps of skin hanging from every limb would suffocate his hapless victim, whom he would then tear apart and eat raw, since he lacked basic fire-making skills. Garkain, like Namorodo, is something of an exception among Australian spirits. The vast majority are harmless, no threat to the people they, in any case only seldom, meet: the anthill-man of Arnhem Land's western uplands is more common.

Indolence and Evil

Buma-Buma lives alone in a giant termite mound, from which he never ventures very far. Though he has mastered all the arts and equipment of

Aboriginal hunting, and a knowledge of fire, he is far too indolent to bother using them. Instead he lives on honey he gathers from hives, and catches small lizards and anteaters: larger game than this, he feels, is altogether too much trouble.

Yet if placid spirits like Buma-Buma are more typical than grotesque monsters such as Garkain, human nature being what it is the dangerous spirits receive more than their fair share of mythic attention. What story-teller could resist the thought of Milinjee, knock-kneed nocturnal killer of the Djauan people, who has sharp stone blades on each elbow and burning eyes in his demonic face?

A neighbouring tribe, from the Roper Valley, tell of Nanmamnrootmee, a place infested by evil

Dozens of termite mounds dot the landscape near Tennant Creek, reminders of the chosen home of Buma-Buma, a benign spirit more concerned with easy living than harming humans.

The Medicine People

Bridging the gap between the dead and the living, shamans obtained their magic during dream-like trances. Their gifts might be curative or predictive – whichever, they could be powerful.

Belief in the shaman's abilities was shared by all Aboriginal peoples. Although ordinary enough in most aspects of his life he had been taken in charge by the dead medicine-men of the past. He was inducted into all the healing and divining arts, and when he grew up, married and had children, and hunted with his fellow men, he kept company with the ancestors all the while. They came to him as he slept, some said, and, endowing him with an eagle's form, bore him off night after night to their world to receive instruction. In other traditions the future medicine-man might fall into a trance after wandering off into the desert, or climb up the body of a Rainbow Snake into the sky. Whatever form it took, this was the invisible education through which such men gained their powers.

spirits ever since the time when the devil-woman Marm sat there grinding plums on a rock one day. Marm was eyeless, but she worked by unfailing touch, grinding huge quantities of plums which girls brought to her. By the time she had finished she had worn a round hole in the stone, and prepared a feast of juicy plum-pulp for her helpers. No sooner had they eaten, however, than they lost their human form, being transformed into a host of dancing devils. Marm's millstone and the fruit-pulp remains, now turned to stone, can be seen in the valley to this day. Harder to spot, yet still ubiquitous, are the she-devils she brought into being, whose siren voices summon the unwary traveller.

Nabonkitkit the Loner

Nabonkitkit was a demon recalled by the Djauan who had two lizards which he kept hidden in the Outback. His younger brother Kimurree found them one day when out hunting on his own: he bore them home proudly and showed them to Nabonkitkit. He was astonished and upset when his brother told him he was too young to keep them, but Kimurree tightened his lip and held his peace. Next time they went out hunting, however, he got his revenge by telling Nabonkitkit he had seen an eagle's nest on top of a tree. Nabonkitkit climbed all day without making any real progress: the higher he ascended the more distant the eyrie seemed. Only gradually did it dawn on him that his brother had charmed the tree into growing: what was worse, he had tied a knot in its trunk so he could not get down. Kimurree went off laughing in triumph: his pompous brother would die up there, he said, while he himself would go home and reclaim his lizards.

Nabonkitkit stayed aloft through the wet season and on through the dry, until finally a chill winter wind blew him down – his fall was far, but he just dusted himself down. He ate every plant and crawling creature, every bird and animal he could find, until very soon the flesh and muscles of his body had been restored to normal. Quiet and unflustered, yet implacably vengeful, Nabonkitkit then hunted down his brother. When he found him he wielded his stone axe and dispatched both Kimurree and his lizards: from here on, he said, he would do without companions of any kind, making his way in the world all alone.

Death's Inevitability

Death may be the universal destiny of humankind, but as originally created all living things were intended to live forever. That death should have arisen in the first place, and then later become permanent, were the result of people's own obstinacy and selfishness.

An ancestor of the Worora people of the western Kimberleys, Widjingara was the first man to die. He was killed by an enemy come to steal a woman who had been promised to one of his own tribe. Widjingara sprang to the woman's assistance and paid for his heroism with his life. On hearing of his death, Widjingara's wife, the black-headed python-woman, shaved her hair and painted herself with ashes, yet she seemed to care more for these rituals themselves than for the loss of her husband. Sparing no ceremony, she placed him in a bark coffin, had him laid to rest, then began an exhibitionistic display of grief.

As was the way of the dead in the Dreamtime days, he was soon up and about again, none the worse for his experience. Returning home to his widow, he greeted her cheerily – yet his reception was not as he had hoped. Far from rejoicing to see him, his snake-wife snapped at him: What on earth did he think he was doing here? Had she not just shaved off all her hair and daubed herself from head to foot in ash?

His reappearance had plainly made a mockery of her mourning, and now it was Widjingara's turn to be angry: he stalked off back to his grave where this time he resolved to stay. From thenceforth death would be a permanent condition for all, not the strange state of indeterminacy it had been, and funeral practices were amended accordingly. Rather than being preserved for the soul's prompt revival, the bodies of the dead would in future be left outside to decay on platforms made of branches and to be picked over by wild beasts. The bare bones would then be laid to rest in a

Funeral Poles of the Tiwi

Strange poles stick out of the earth in the graveyards of the Tiwi people of Bathurst Island. Elaborately carved and richly painted in an amazing array of stylized forms, they mark the continuing existence after death of the dreaming deceased.

Here there are no dates or descriptions, as might be found on a Western headstone, but the images stacked up in this vertical record constitute a full account of the departed's identity as it would be appreciated in Aboriginal terms. Not only are his totemic animals and special plants recorded, but the landscape in which he hunted and the house in which he lived. All that was essential to his being is thus captured here for all to see – almost as if he had never died at all.

A painted human form on a Bathurst Island Tiwi *pukamani* burial pole. The departing soul will stop to say farewell.

cave or buried. Widjingara, ironically, would be an exception to this new rule, not in fact remaining in his coffin for very long at all, despite his promise. Instead his spirit was reincarnated in the form of the native cat, a notorious scavenger on human carrion, often seen on burial platforms in close communion with the freshly laid-out corpse.

The Tiwi people of Melville Island, off the continent's northern coast, have a different version of how death first came about. They tell of how their founding ancestor Purukupali lost his son Jinini when he was just a baby boy. His mother Bima had neglected him, too busy having an affair

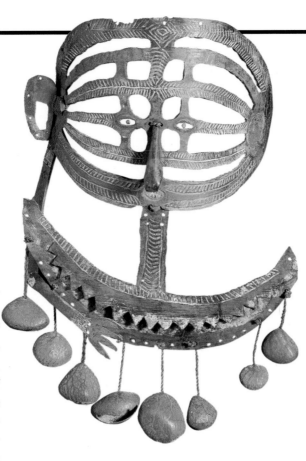

Torres Strait turtleshell mask with rattles made of nut husks, *c.*19th century. Emblematic of the culture heroes, such items were used in funerary ceremonies.

with her lover Japara. Grief-stricken by the boy's death and by his wife's twofold betrayal, Purukupali beat both her and Japara to a bloody pulp. Despite this Japara felt sympathy for his rival and offered to restore his son to life. Purukupali refused, picked up the boy's body and walked out into the sea with it until both were lost to sight.

Drowning himself, in his pain and anger he condemned all who came after to a similar fate: from now on, he said, death without hope of physical resurrection would be the common lot of all. A whirlpool in the Dundas Strait marks the place where he disappeared, still a death-trap for the unwary navigator to this day. As for Japara, he rose into the sky to become the moon, the scars of his beating still visible on his face. Powerful as he was he could not escape Purukupali's curse entirely, but though dying every month, he gets resurrected (see page 70).

Widjingara's death was caused in the first instance by the aggression of others; its perpetuation was the result of his own petulance and spite. Purukupali's obstinacy not only brought about his death but made him spurn Japara's offer to bring his beloved child back to life.

Celebration

Although now seen as inevitable, Aborigines see no reason for death to be a source of terror. Those approaching death will not cease to be, but merely pass from one level of existence to another. Their spirit joining those of ancestors who went on before them, they will remain in close contact with those they are leaving behind. The Yellow Ochre Dance celebrates the bond between the deceased and their living descendants; sand sculptures too are created to underline the links between those alive and the dreaming dead.

There is duality in death, however: two separate souls leave the spent body, so that while the *birrimbirr* lingers among the living, the *mokuy* journeys to an afterworld. Sometimes this is a Heaven among the stars; sometimes it is a distant island or a far-off continent. Among the Aborigines of Arnhem Land the dead are thought to journey to the isle of Purelko, paddled there by Wulawait, the spectral boatman. An honour guard of dolphins bears the *mokuy* on its voyage far beyond the rising sun. A masked plover, which has followed its progress, at the last flies on ahead to warn the other spirits of the soul's approach.

ANCESTRAL DANCES

Colourful painting of parts of the body was used in much of the Oceania region, both as an art in its own right and to complement tattooing designs. The decorations reflected the wearers' prestige and power. In New Guinea men usually wore the most complex designs, taking prominent roles in public displays to emphasize their social and spiritual status. Elaborate decoration was associated with the concept of *mana*, or spiritual power, which was often considered to be a force or substance inherited from divine ancestors. Objects, dress or dance could thus link the dancers with their dead forbears at various occasions of family or tribal importance.

Above: **Sing-sing dancers in New Guinea paint the different sides of their bodies white and black for a dramatic two-tone effect.**

Above: A participant dressed for the traditional Crocodile Dance in Sepik, New Guinea. The crocodile is the ancestral animal totem of one of the Sepik River region's tribes, and the animal features in the decoration of men's houses and various ritual paraphernalia. An origin myth from the area relates that the world floats on the back of a crocodile. By dressing in this way, therefore, the dancer can embody the power and invoke the help of the deity.

Above, right: An ornately decorated participant in the Festival of Pacific Arts, the region's biggest cultural event. New Guinea is blessed with a large and fantastical array of colourful bird species and is the only home of the magnificent Bird of Paradise, whose feathers have long featured prominently in dance and ritual.

Left: New Guinea mudmen from the Eastern Highlands wearing their dancing masks. Traditionally, the mudmen performed to encourage their own warriors while frightening the enemy. The grey colour of the clay masks, and the earth which is smeared on their bodies, are both associated with death and the spirit world.

THE MYRIAD BELIEFS OF MELANESIA

In 1521 Ferdinand de Magellan landed on the Micronesian island of Guam. It was a fleeting contact but it began a process that had disastrous repercussions for the native populations of the region, scattering its people and all but wiping its mythology off the map.

The same blessing was visited on Melanesia, to the south. Centred on the massive bulk of New Guinea, the islands harboured elements of Australian, Micronesian and Polynesian mythology. They also had legends of their own, linked by a way of life that reflected their diverse cultures. Although no better equipped than Micronesia to withstand the Western onslaught, Melanesia's size prevented it from being overwhelmed.

New Guinea was a land of topographical contrasts inhabited by various peoples whose many tribes, clans and septs spoke a host of different dialects. On its own New Guinea provided a rich enough mythological stew. But there was more to Melanesia than that. Around New Guinea circled a group of island archipelagoes – the Solomons, Vanuatu and others – each of which added its own spice to the pot. Far to the east, meanwhile, Fiji contributed a dash of Polynesian flavouring.

The distinguishing feature of Melanesia, if such a place could be said to have one, was its individuality. There was no unifying pantheon of gods – although elements of such a thing existed in Fiji. Instead, each community revered its own deity or, more often, a culture hero. These latter were spirits or distant ancestors who had created the basics of Melanesian existence – food, sex, death, agriculture, fishing and houses, for example. They were widely believed to remain alive in the world and were honoured with elaborate ceremonies, with accompanying myths, which by tradition were known only to a select group of initiates. To address the same spirit it was not uncommon for the men of one tribe to follow one set of protocols while the women obeyed another. This regime of exclusivity pervaded Melanesia to the extent that only rarely was a spirit recognized by neighbouring tribes, let alone throughout an island, an archipelago or the whole region.

Left: A *karawari* female ancestor figure, from New Guinea. It was believed that through the arts the spirits visited this world and maintained ties between the dead and the living.

Opposite: The Solomon Islands, one of the larger archipelagoes which make up the region of Melanesia. They were named by the Spanish explorer Alvaro de Mendana after the Biblical king because he hoped to find gold there.

81

Life and the Loss of Immortality

Melanesians had few myths to explain the creation of the world or the universe. Earth had always existed, providing a fertile seedbed from which sprang humans, plants, fish and animals. What they lacked on a grand scale, however, they more than made up for in the details. Few areas contained such a plethora of tales concerning the arrival of humans.

Humans came to Melanesia from a score of different sources. They were created from wood, mud or sand. They sprang from plants, eggs, stones, fleas and even bloodclots. Occasionally, they simply erupted from the ground.

Sometimes their arrival was spontaneous. In the Admiralty Islands, for example, humankind hatched from an egg laid by a primeval turtle. In a story that uncannily pre-empted the theory of evolutionary mutation, it was said that the turtle laid a large clutch of eggs in the sand, some of which produced turtles but others of which opened to reveal the first men and women. In a similarly naturalistic vein, it was believed in New Britain that humans had budded from a plant; a variation of the theme among the Papuans in New Guinea recounted how man came from the soil and woman from a tree.

Very often, however, humankind was created by a pre-existent being. In Micronesia, which was influenced by the more structured mythology of Polynesia, it was said that men and women owed their origins to a god and a goddess who were the first inhabitants of the world. The god made a man and the goddess made a woman, thereby creating the first couple from whom all later humans were descended. Other myths ascribed the human genesis to a goddess who became pregnant and gave birth to children from her eyes.

These views were not restricted solely to Micronesia. In New Britain the Baining tribe believed that the first beings were the sun and the moon. They mated to produce stones and birds, some of which became men and women respectively. Elsewhere in New Britain an originating deity created the first two men, one of whom, in turn, created the first two women from coconuts. In a further elaboration, one of the coconuts was dark and one light, thereby explaining why Papuans had darker skin than their fairer Melanesian neighbours.

Occasionally, design and spontaneity intermingled. In the southwest of New Guinea, the Keraki people held that human life originated in

the ubiquitous palm trees that fringed their shores. It was Gainji, the first being, who strolled through the palms and heard noises emanating from a tree. He listened and found that it was speech. Very carefully he removed the speaking creatures and set them on the earth, dividing them into groups that could understand each other. In doing so he not only liberated humankind but created the linguistic diversity that characterizes New Guinea.

Life's Certain Companion: Death

Just as life had many interpretations, so did its inescapable bedfellow death. The first humans were immortal, or at the least regenerating, like the stones and trees from which they had been born. Death came about either through a quarrel between the gods or, in some parts of Micronesia, because the god who intended to create humans was searching for the elixir of immortality and in his absence a lesser god created men and women without the necessary ingredient. In Vanuatu life was likened to a snake's skin, being shed regularly in a process of renewal. Death came about because humans either neglected to shed their skins or because their old skin, into which they would later climb, had been irreparably damaged. In one story the skin was destroyed by children at play – an uncomfortable reminder of the way in which children mirror their own parents' mortality.

A painted panel of palm-leaf from a Sepik house facade in New Guinea. These colourful figures represent clan-specific ancestral spirits. All houses had ghost owners who had to be propitiated.

Deeds of the Heroes

In the absence of a structured pantheon, Melanesian mythology embraced a host of culture heroes who were instrumental in making the world the way it was. Very often these were two brothers, one wise and the other foolish. Sometimes, however, the hero was a single being who roamed the islands, stamping his mark on topography and society alike.

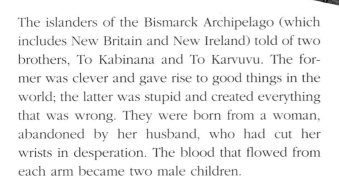

The islanders of the Bismarck Archipelago (which includes New Britain and New Ireland) told of two brothers, To Kabinana and To Karvuvu. The former was clever and gave rise to good things in the world; the latter was stupid and created everything that was wrong. They were born from a woman, abandoned by her husband, who had cut her wrists in desperation. The blood that flowed from each arm became two male children.

As they grew to maturity, the boys planted coconuts to create women with whom they could breed. To Karvuvu, however, planted his coconut upside down and produced a race of women whose noses had an ugly depression instead of a prominent bridge. To Karvuvu's incompetence was never-ending: he tried to make fish but only created a shark; and he also helped bring about humankind's mortality. When his mother grew old and wrinkled she shed her skin in order to become young again. But To Karvuvu did not recognize her and became so distressed that she resumed her old skin, thus ending the cycle of regeneration humankind had previously been blessed with.

Brotherly Rivals

The theme of two hostile brothers was common-place throughout Melanesia. Frequently their rivalry reached such a pitch that the clever one

An incised shark from the Santa Cruz Islands in the Solomons provides a reminder of To Karvuvu's incompetent creation.

would try to murder the other. The usual method of dispatch was to bury the victim in the foundations of a new structure. The designated grave was typically the hole into which the main supporting post was to be lowered. Inevitably, however, the would-be victim escaped and continued to bedevil the world with his incompetence.

In one version, the Solomon Islanders replaced the two brothers with a band of male siblings. The youngest was different from the rest. Born with his umbilical cord wrapped around his neck – a sign of supernatural power – he was precociously intelligent and immediately wanted to know what his brothers were doing. Dashing off, he found them struggling to erect the ridgepole of a boathouse. Because he had passed a dog with its ears pricked, he told his brothers to carve the pole in the dog's likeness. They did so, but were infuriated at the advice coming from one so young. When they next built a house the younger brother not only offered his advice but single-handedly uprooted a tree to act as the main post. Driven to

Swan Maidens

Many culture heroes found their wives in the sky. The swan maidens story was widespread throughout Melanesia and the main character could be Qat, Tangaro or sometimes – as among Vanuatu's Efate people – a simple human.

There was a divine race of women who visited Earth in the guise of swans. They came down at night, when the tide was out, and discarded their wings to go fishing. When dawn came and the tide turned they would pick up their wings and fly home. One night, however, a man saw them at work. He stole a pair of wings which he buried under the main post of his house. Come daybreak the swan maidens flew home – all save one beautiful woman who could not find her wings. The man seized her and made her his wife. They had two children, both boys, whose names were Tafaki and Karisi Bum.

In time, however, the man grew tired of his wife and began to beat her. She wept bitter tears that washed away the earth floor of their home. The more she wept the more the soil ran away until, one day, she spotted the wings her husband had hidden. She put them on and flew up to the sky, telling her sons to find her when they were able.

The boys became rich and clever men. Their powers were such that they climbed a palm tree armed with clubs in order to beat the winds into submission. Although unsuccessful, they managed nevertheless to turn the southwest wind into a whimpering, soon-forgotten thing.

When the two sons were out hunting they fired an arrow at a bird flying high in the sky. It missed its target and hit a celestial banyan tree. They fired more arrows, each of which hit the other until there was a chain leading down to Earth. Climbing up it, they discovered not their swan-maiden mother but their blind grandmother, who was tending yams. They were able to cure her blindness and descended the arrow-ladder with a basket containing her thanks: pigs, fowl, yams and every plant that could possibly be of use to humankind.

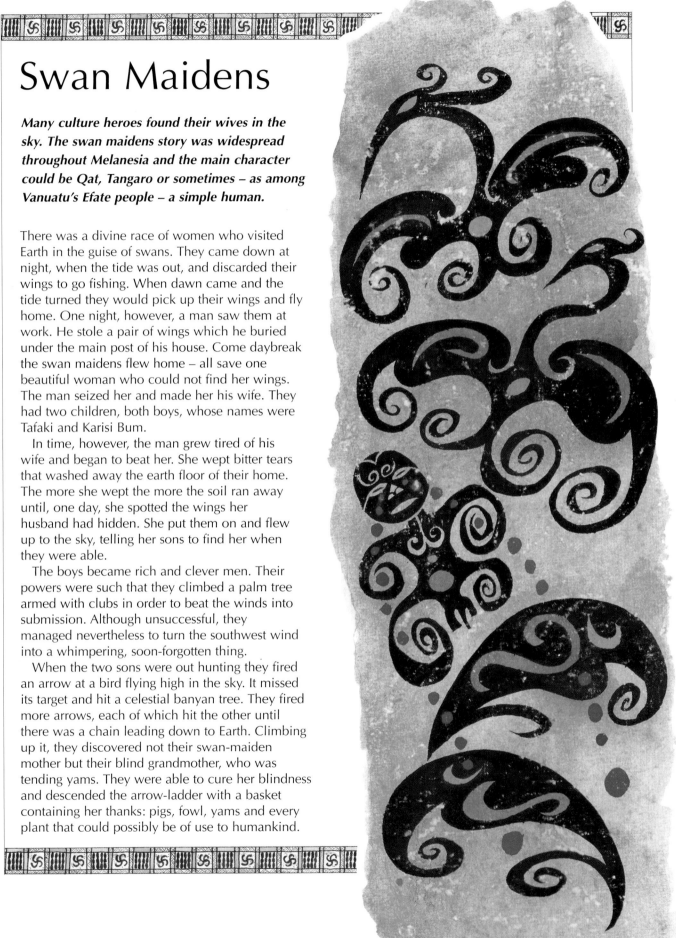

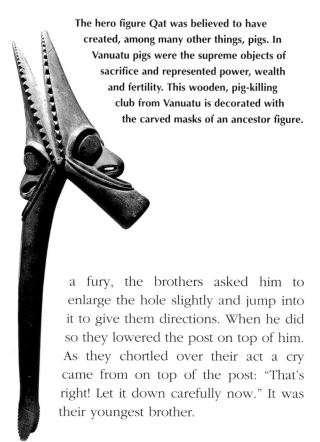

The hero figure Qat was believed to have created, among many other things, pigs. In Vanuatu pigs were the supreme objects of sacrifice and represented power, wealth and fertility. This wooden, pig-killing club from Vanuatu is decorated with the carved masks of an ancestor figure.

a fury, the brothers asked him to enlarge the hole slightly and jump into it to give them directions. When he did so they lowered the post on top of him. As they chortled over their act a cry came from on top of the post: "That's right! Let it down carefully now." It was their youngest brother.

Qat's Labours

One of the greatest of all the brother-myth figures was the hero Qat. A good-natured character from Vanuatu's Banks Islands, Qat was viewed simultaneously as a spirit and as an ancestor. Born from a large rock, he was the eldest of eleven brothers, the other ten all being called Tangaro. He was credited with creating men, pigs, trees, rocks and everything of importance on Earth – not according to any grand plan but just as the fancy took him. Try as he might, however, the one thing that Qat could not create was night. Eventually he heard that darkness could be obtained from a being called I Qong who lived on Vava Island in the Torres Strait. Setting off with a large pig, he succeeded in purchasing the gift of night. Not only that, but he brought back birds so that men would know when daybreak was due. Far from being pleased, his brothers were disturbed – even if it meant a rest from their labours, sleep resembled death too closely for their liking. Qat promised that

the loss of consciousness would only be temporary and that the birds would wake them. They submitted reluctantly and Qat unleashed the first night. Towards morning he heard the birds singing and knew the time was ripe for a new day. Taking a piece of red obsidian he sliced along the eastern horizon to reveal the rising sun.

Instead of his brothers, Qat was sometimes accompanied by a companion called Marawa who was both maverick obstructor and guardian angel. When Qat created humans he carved them out of wood, buried them for three days, then dug them up and for another three days beguiled them into life with drums and music. Marawa, who took the form of a spider, tried to copy him but succeeded only in creating death. He buried his wooden figures not for three days but the full six. When he retrieved them they were rotting and lifeless.

In another tale, Marawa was a wood spirit who did his best to prevent Qat felling a tree to build the first canoe. No matter how hard Qat chopped, Marawa replaced every chip that flew from the trunk. Not until Qat trapped one of the chips did Marawa agree to help in the task. From then on he became Qat's protector and saved him from many disasters. Qat's end came when he had a canoe-building competition with a similar hero from the Trobriand Islands. Both commenced their task inland, far from the shore, and both found their way to the sea by magic. The Trobriander's canoe flew; Qat's meanwhile, ploughed a channel through the earth. When Qat reached the ocean he did not stop but disappeared across the waves forever, taking with him many of the Earth's best things. Ironically, when the first white men arrived with their trinkets and their

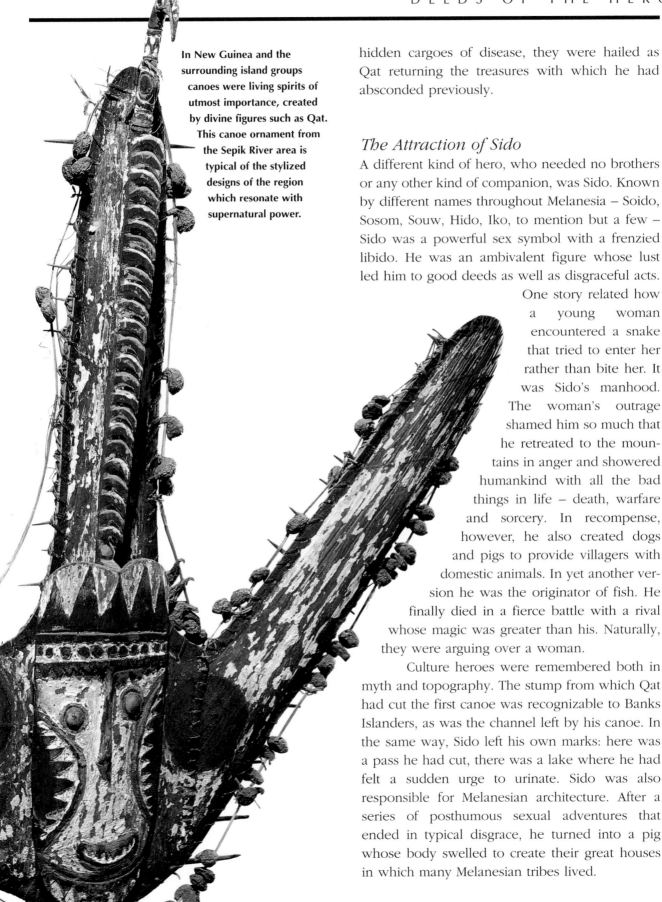

In New Guinea and the surrounding island groups canoes were living spirits of utmost importance, created by divine figures such as Qat. This canoe ornament from the Sepik River area is typical of the stylized designs of the region which resonate with supernatural power.

hidden cargoes of disease, they were hailed as Qat returning the treasures with which he had absconded previously.

The Attraction of Sido

A different kind of hero, who needed no brothers or any other kind of companion, was Sido. Known by different names throughout Melanesia – Soido, Sosom, Souw, Hido, Iko, to mention but a few – Sido was a powerful sex symbol with a frenzied libido. He was an ambivalent figure whose lust led him to good deeds as well as disgraceful acts. One story related how a young woman encountered a snake that tried to enter her rather than bite her. It was Sido's manhood. The woman's outrage shamed him so much that he retreated to the mountains in anger and showered humankind with all the bad things in life – death, warfare and sorcery. In recompense, however, he also created dogs and pigs to provide villagers with domestic animals. In yet another version he was the originator of fish. He finally died in a fierce battle with a rival whose magic was greater than his. Naturally, they were arguing over a woman.

Culture heroes were remembered both in myth and topography. The stump from which Qat had cut the first canoe was recognizable to Banks Islanders, as was the channel left by his canoe. In the same way, Sido left his own marks: here was a pass he had cut, there was a lake where he had felt a sudden urge to urinate. Sido was also responsible for Melanesian architecture. After a series of posthumous sexual adventures that ended in typical disgrace, he turned into a pig whose body swelled to create their great houses in which many Melanesian tribes lived.

A World of Men and Women

Heroes such as Qat and Sido were widely known. At the same time, every society venerated figures who were integral to its own way of life. In New Guinea, the people of Tangu compiled a series of tales centred on the hero-spirits Paki and Dumban.

Originally, Paki was the only being who knew how to sow seeds and cultivate fields. While he lived in plenty other humans eked out a meagre existence as scavengers, feeding off the bark of trees, seeds, roots and whatever else they could find in the forest. One day, however, a human picked up a rotten banana that Paki had discarded and tried to plant it. It failed. Taking pity on the man's incompetence, Paki hung his next harvest on a huge pole that stretched up to the tallest tree and promised humans that if they managed to cut down the pole they could have everything on it. The task was more difficult than it seemed, for no matter how ferociously the humans hewed by day the pole magically repaired itself by night. By chance, one chip flew out and stuck in a man's leg. Thinking no more

A stylized Sepik figure of a spirit known as a *yipwon* that assists men in hunting and headhunting. It is kept in the men's house and hidden from women and the uninitiated. The hooks represent the body: the two central ones are ribs and the middle piece is the heart.

of it, he flung it in the fire. The following morning the pole was perfect save for one chip. Learning from this experience, the men burned all the chips they cut from the pole and, in due course, managed to cut it in two. Even then, however, the pole did not fall down. It was held up by a length of cane attaching it to a nearby tree.

A boy was sent up to cut the pole free, but when he reached the cane it began to speak: "It is I, Paki, not just an ordinary piece of cane you are trying to cut. You cannot cut me! But you tell all those men and women down there to pleasure each other – and then you'll see!" The boy was too embarrassed to repeat Paki's message, so told his elders he had been unable to cut the cane because a bee was troubling him. A second boy was sent up but he too came down with a mumbled excuse. Finally, a third, more experienced boy was found who was not ashamed to shout down Paki's instructions. The people did as they were told and the pole came tumbling down, showering the earth with every crop imaginable.

The cornucopia was wasted. Understanding nothing about the opportunity with which Paki had presented them, the humans simply ate the food. Only two people – an orphaned brother and sister – retained their shares in the hope that they might be able to make something of them. Paki was pleased by their foresight and visited them in a dream to show them how to grow crops. He told them how to choose the right soil, how to plant seeds, how to tend them and harvest them and how to prepare the ground for the following season – each activity being strictly allocated to either male or female. He also taught them a ritual to ensure future prosperity: they must make love on

The Act of Initiation

Throughout Melanesia, a person's cultural progress was marked by initiation ceremonies. They celebrated events such as a boy's nose-piercing, his ear-piercing and his marriage as well as a number of important "firsts" ranging from the gathering of a yam to the killing of another human.

"Naven" ceremonies, as they were known among the Iatmul of New Guinea, drew children into the world of their elders. Each boy or girl would be sponsored by a *wau* – a spiritual overseer from a related clan – who would be responsible for recognizing their deeds and celebrating them appropriately. Minor acts, such as making the first journey from one village to another, might be recognized merely by throwing a handful of lime over the child and chanting a list of ancestors. Major steps, however, received more elaborate rewards in the form of feasts and dances where the participants would wear masks and present gifts to the initiate. Naven ceremonies had their bloody side. They could be conducted on the occasion of a homicide or of collusion in a fatality. A youth who paddled a war canoe or who lured a stranger to his death was considered almost as worthy as the man who performed the act of killing. But they also honoured touchingly domestic events. A group of children who managed to fell their first palm tree, the boys cutting open the trunk and the girls washing its pith, were considered as worthy of Naven as the bravest warriors.

A young boy is painted up by an older man for a rite. Body decoration, either permanent or temporary, played an important part in expressing power.

the ground to be cultivated and then dig in the spilled semen along with a concoction of coconut milk, bark shavings and blood. The brother and sister followed his instructions and thrived. They became the parents of all farmers – but those who had squandered Paki's gift died.

Why Women Fish

Human fecundity, and the division of roles, was linked intimately to agricultural fertility. The same theme was expressed in the story of Dumban whose irresistible allure explained why women went fishing and also gave rise to some of New Guinea's lustier male rituals. Dumban was an insatiable Lothario who rose one day from the river to make love to a woman who had cast her net into the water. Word spread of Dumban's abilities and before long all the women were down by the river's edge. All they needed to do was cast their nets and Dumban would emerge. Soon they were all lying by the riverbank and enjoying themselves so much that they forgot to bring back any fish. At this their husbands became suspicious. They followed their wives to the river. On seeing Dumban they were so angry that they cut him into pieces, leaving only his penis, which was preserved by the women. The penis flew across New Guinea, enjoying itself at every settlement, until it finally sank from sight in a river pool. Two boys heard its chant of virility and repeated it to their elders. Ever since then women fished while their men sang Dumban's song and conducted elaborate ceremonies to demonstrate their prowess.

Respect for the Animals

The teeming wildlife of Melanesia – particularly of the larger islands such as New Guinea – played a major part in the region's mythology. Animals were often considered the living representations of supernatural beings – gods, spirits or dead ancestors – and were treated with according respect, with the pig perhaps the most esteemed of all.

In many parts of Melanesia and Micronesia the largest land mammal was the pig. Not only a source of food it was also an object of veneration. The Kiwais of New Guinea believed that the first pig was created by Marunogere, a culture hero akin to Qat and Sido, who gave humankind, among other things, the secret of building houses – until then they had lived in miserable holes in the ground.

The pig was born when Marunogere passed a solid lump of undigested sago that he was inspired to make into something useful. He gave it a coconut stalk for a tail and used coconut fibres for its hair. Its teeth were made from the white flesh of the coconut and the nut's sprouting end became its snout. It required only the coconut's notches for eyes and the first pig was ready.

Marunogere's actions neatly linked three basic food sources: sago, pork and coconuts. They also bore architectural fruit: the houses that he taught humans to build had a pig's trotter buried at each corner, a pig's jaw laid under the entrance and a pig's skull hoisted above the lintel. The pig's vertebrae and ribs were scattered across the roofbeams.

Such was the importance of pigs that according to one legend they had almost ruled the Earth. The people of Efate in Vanuatu held that it was a close call as to whether humans or pigs should be the supreme creature. Only after letting the two species loose did the divine authorities make a decision. Seeing how the pigs spent their time rootling for food night and day, paying no attention to the hungry humans, the gods demoted them to animal status for being too selfish. Elsewhere, it was believed that Qat (see page 86) had originally made humans and pigs in the same mould but had relegated pigs to walk on all fours following the protestation of his brothers.

Pigs were closely linked to the supernatural: they could see phenomena invisible to man; they acted as repositories for divine spirits; they had their own souls; sometimes they could also contain the souls of dead humans. On Fiji a select number of pigs

Decorated Solomon Islands paddle. Frigate birds are a common theme and represent ancestral spirits. Here, they show the spirits of the drowned returned to advise the living fishermen. A bird-man is at top right.

was reserved for sacrificial use only. Feeding these consecrated creatures was an act of piety that helped settle the spirits of the departed.

Sometimes, however, pigs were shunned. Solomon Islanders lived in terror of a hideous demon boar, which had a flat head and a hornet's nest hanging from its jaw. The very sight of this wild pig was enough to ensure a man's death. Sometimes the boar would be accompanied by a herd of equally malevolent swine who could wipe out whole villages. There was no escape from these creatures, for as they approached a settlement they shrank to the size of mice and were able to slip in unnoticed. It is possible that people may have used the myth to explain epidemic diseases that had no apparent cause.

Snake: Life-Giver and Life-Threatener

Pigs were not the only animals to be respected. The Solomon Islanders believed that sharks, dogs and hawks also possessed souls. The people of Motu, on New Guinea, considered frogs to be spirits: should one enter a house, it was a sure sign of impending death. The Kiwais, meanwhile, claimed that birds had once been able to speak and that some of their calls still resembled human speech. On the Trobriand Islands, sailors lived in fear of a gigantic octopus whose tentacles could reach up to becalm a canoe; their grip could be loosened only by a prompt – and often human – sacrifice.

No creature, however, loomed so large in Melanesian imagination as the snake. In New Guinea it was a snake god called Randalo who had saved humankind from a devastating flood. The waters grew higher and higher, driving people before them until there was only a small band of survivors huddled atop the highest peak. Randalo emerged from the mountaintop and came to his people's defence. Hissing, and spitting out his forked tongue, he forced the ocean to retreat until it once more lapped the beaches. Never again did the waves dare threaten the snake god's realm.

In many areas snakes were seen as creators. The inhabitants of the Florida Islands in the Solomons group worshipped a female snake spirit called Koevasi from whom all humans were born. She also taught humans the secrets of speech but, alas, she was suffering at the time from a fever. In copying her confused sounds the Floridans ended up with a variety of dialects. On San Cristobal in the Solomons the creator was a winged snake called Hatuibwari who possessed a human head, four eyes and four breasts. In some places, however, he was considered a manifestation of an even more powerful snake, Agunua. It was said that Agunua had created all things on Earth, but had suffered a number of initial setbacks. His brother, for example, had burned a number of vegetables and fruits in the oven, thereby making them forever inedible. And when Agunua created the first man, he found him so incapable of looking after himself that he had to create woman as well.

The snake was seen both as a life-giving and a life-threatening force, and as such was widely regarded as the controller of rain: in a good mood it would dispense the moisture necessary for agriculture; when provoked it would unleash destructive deluges.

A totemic figure from New Ireland displaying a bird and a shark, both were respected animals believed by different Melanesian tribes to possess souls.

A Fijian Hierarchy

Situated in the easternmost corner of Melanesia, the Fiji Islands were also influenced by the mythology of the neighbouring Polynesia region. While embracing the cultural heroes found throughout Melanesia, Fijians also believed in a more structured hierarchy of gods who had ordered life on Earth.

An important deity was the god Ndengei, a being who was half-snake and half-stone. It was he who had created humans from two eggs that had been laid near his home by a hawk. Admiring the eggs' beauty, he decided to hatch them himself and in due course they produced a boy and a girl. He set them on either side of a large vesi tree where, after six years, they finally discovered each other and became the ancestors of the human race. Ndengei was so taken by his creations that he supplied them with bananas, yams and taro. Then, seeing that they could only eat the bananas, he gave them the gift of fire so that they could cook the other two plants.

A lagoon in Fiji, an island chain situated in eastern Melanesia that has influences from Melanesia and Polynesia.

In some accounts, however, Ndengei was a slightly incompetent creator. It took him several goes before he formed an acceptable-looking man. As for women, his first attempt was so disastrous that his son Rokomuto was quite appalled when he met her. He rebuked his father soundly and made some pertinent suggestions whereby women were recreated in their present form.

Ndengei – working through Rokomotu – also created Fiji's rugged topography. Acting on his father's instructions, Rokomotu first made rough lumps of land that he scraped up from the seabed, then strode across the islands to give them shape. Wherever he let his feather cloak trail behind him it produced smooth, sandy beaches. When he hitched it up, he left rocky shores and mountains in his wake. The landscape was never entirely stable, however, for Ndengei tended to move about as he slept in his cave on Kauvandra Mountain. Whenever he did so he caused one of the terrifying earthquakes to which Fiji was highly vulnerable.

As a creator, Ndengei was also associated with flood myths. It was said that night fell when Ndengei slept and day came when he was awoken by a black dove. The arrangement was accepted by all save his two nephews, who worked as boatbuilders. Wearying of their toil, they decided to earn some extra sleep by killing the black dove. Their actions served only to rouse Ndengei's wrath. He brought down a fearsome deluge of rain that overwhelmed the two brothers and swept them and their families across the islands. The flood brought the secret of boatbuilding to every tribe on Fiji; it also condemned boatbuilders never to be their own masters but always the servants of chiefs.

In a theme that was common throughout Melanesia, Ndengei had a divine opponent who worked to undo his good deeds. On some islands the battle between good and evil was represented by the spirit Tagaroa – associated with the powerful Polynesian deity Tangaroa – and his nemesis,

Suqe. On Fiji, Ndengei's counterpart was a god named Ove. Whereas Ndengei wanted everything to turn out well, Ove wished everything for the worst. It was thanks to Ove that disease and disaster visited the islands and that humans were born malformed. An immortal being who represented the dark side of creation, Ove strove continually to cause trouble.

Whatever travails they suffered thanks to Ove's machinations, all Fijians looked forward to life after death in the afterworld, Mbulu. Belief in an afterworld was widespread throughout Melanesia. Typically it lay to the west – towards the setting sun and the mainland from which they had first migrated – and was sited on a distant island, on the seabed or, occasionally, in the sky. But these afterworlds were nebulous places and only on Fiji was the concept expanded. Humans, it was believed, had two souls: a dark and a fair one. On death the fair soul would linger by the body as a ghost that could take human form when it wished. Meanwhile the dark soul journeyed to Mbulu. It travelled to the northwest of the island, to the mouth of Ndengei's cave – and from there it descended to the shore and was carried by a divine ferryman to a far-off town. Here it would be judged by a mortal, Samu, "Killer of Souls", who tested the soul in combat to ensure it was worthy of admittance to the final court of Ndengei. Perched atop a high precipice over whose edge protruded a long oar, Ndengei weeded out the boastful and vainglorious. Anyone caught exaggerating his past deeds was congratulated and invited to take a seat on the paddle of the oar. No sooner had the soul made itself comfortable than Ndengei's helpers tipped it onto the rocks below. Those who passed interrogation were allowed to stand by the oar's handle before departing to the place in which they had died to be consecrated as ancestral spirits.

Mbulu was not a perfect place. Unlike other Melanesian hereafters, which were welcoming havens where a soul could live in a state of perpetual youth, entry to Mbulu was subject to rigid conditions. Married men were never completely happy unless joined by the souls of their wives – who were often strangled to accompany them – and bachelors had no chance whatsoever of entering Mbulu. Before they even left Fiji they had to brave a fearsome hag and if they escaped her clutches they then had to face a demon named Nanggangga, who sat on a large black rock by the shore and dared them to get past him. No bachelor ever got as far as the ferryman who would take him to Mbulu.

Many of those who reached Mbulu had no special cause to rejoice, for the Fijian afterworld was an extension of life on Earth. Those who had been prosperous continued to be so; those who had been poor lived on likewise. Worse still, the soul was an exact replica of the human at the point of his or her death. Faced with this prospect, many Fijians chose to be buried alive or strangled rather than face an eternity of old age or disease.

Ceremonial oil dish used by the Fijian priestly caste when oiling their bodies prior to ritual performances.

93

Afek the Spirit Heroine

Heroines rarely featured in the male-dominated mythology of Melanesia but Afek, a female spirit, was an exception. In central New Guinea it was believed that she had created everything of importance to society. Afek came alone from the east and out of her string bag dropped food in the form of taro, wealth in the form of nassa shells, and more.

Afek's many gifts were integral to life and religion in New Guinea; thus she became a symbol of procreation and her string bag represented the womb from which life's essentials were born. Besides creating the bare bones of existence Afek also brought into being some of society's more complex codes – among them the segregation of men and women. Traditionally, women were expected to live in one house, looking after the children and livestock, while the men occupied a separate dwelling where they arrayed themselves in ceremonial paint and feathers. In the beginning, these roles were reversed, Afek resided in the male cult house and her brother Umoim was given charge of domestic affairs. It was not a success: the pigs squealed all night and the children ran free. Unable to sleep for the din, Afek suggested they change places. They did so and for the first time everybody enjoyed a good night's rest. The following daybreak Umoim appeared at Afek's door in all his splendour. His skin was rubbed with dew, coated with pork fat and decorated with paint. He wore feathers and had a boar's tusk through his nose. Afek was so delighted at the sight that she decreed that from then on men should garb themselves in finery while women dealt with the mundane chores.

In a more intimate version, the separation of male and female occurred when Afek invented sexual intercourse. Male blood represented force while female menstrual blood represented fertility. Originally men and women had possessed both qualities, but with the advent of reproduction they had to choose which to retain. In forcing them to sacrifice one element of their composition Afek polarized the sexes but at the same time bound them inextricably together.

This mutuality is evident during the important male initiation ceremonies, for it was Afek who created the sacred *bilum* (containing the bones of dead ancestors) which men wear feather versions of on their backs. Male specialists make these *bilums* but they are based on framework designs created by their mothers. Thus each separate form of *bilum* is identified with male or female, one giving a man power, the other underlining the woman's central role. When initiated, the male hears how Afek poisoned Umoim in a ritual to establish a road to the afterworld, but the attempt failed when Umoim became a bird of paradise and disappeared with the road unfinished.

A wooden figure of a clan ancestress from a men's meeting house in New Guinea. Afek established various cult houses during her mythic journeys through the landscape.

Male Prestige

Even in the areas where Afek was venerated, men still claimed the social high ground. Women preserved string bags as objects of ritual significance, the secret of whose construction was passed down the maternal line. But men, too, had their own bags which contained – so they said – myths of origin available only to males.

This freemasonry was echoed throughout Melanesia, resulting in secret societies which acted both as stepping stones to social advancement and repositories of ancient lore. Shrouded in mystery, their proceedings were accompanied by elaborate rituals that were spiritual in intent but which often led to periods of mayhem and debauchery.

In the Banks Islands, male prestige revolved around the Suque, a secret society that involved several grades. An initiate would be proposed by his uncle – to whom he would give a pig – who would then hold a feast for fellow Suque members. Each step up the ladder involved larger payments and increasingly elaborate feasts until the member's status was made plain to all.

The practice was encapsulated in a myth involving a hero called Ganviviris and his sponsor, the sea spirit Ro Som. The sea spirit sponsored Ganviviris so fulsomely that in a single feast he was able to buy his way through two grades of Suque. With Ro Som's help Ganviviris leaped from stage to stage, buying his way with extraordinary pigs whose tusks formed perfect circles.

Once he had reached the top, however, Ganviviris turned his eyes to other Suques, one of which Ro Som had forbidden him to join. Disaster struck: one of Ganviviris's feasts was interrupted by the arrival of a woman smeared with red earth and wearing pigs' tails in her hair. The men looked on aghast as the apparition made her way to Ganviviris's house. No sooner had she entered the door than they rushed after her. But she was gone. And so was Ganviviris's wealth. Unable to maintain his status, Ganviviris was thrown out of the Suque and died five days later.

SANCTUMS OF THE SPIRITS

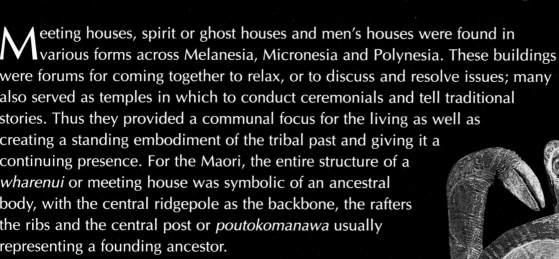

Meeting houses, spirit or ghost houses and men's houses were found in various forms across Melanesia, Micronesia and Polynesia. These buildings were forums for coming together to relax, or to discuss and resolve issues; many also served as temples in which to conduct ceremonials and tell traditional stories. Thus they provided a communal focus for the living as well as creating a standing embodiment of the tribal past and giving it a continuing presence. For the Maori, the entire structure of a *wharenui* or meeting house was symbolic of an ancestral body, with the central ridgepole as the backbone, the rafters the ribs and the central post or *poutokomanawa* usually representing a founding ancestor.

Above: A 19th-century print depicts a Fijian temple or spirit house dedicated to Mbau. The house is distinguished by the chains of white shells decorating its peaked roof.

Left: The Te Hau-Ki-Turanga meeting house was built in 1842 by the Ngati Kaipoho of the Rongowhakaata tribe. The central supporting pole represents a specific founding ancestor who can be identified by his distinctive tattoos.

POLYNESIAN PARADISE

Scattered across thousands of kilometres of Pacific Ocean, in a rough triangle that spans two hemispheres and stretches south from Hawaii to Aotearoa (New Zealand) and east from Tonga to Easter Island, Polynesia occupies one-third of the globe's surface. Historically, it was isolated not only from the outer world but most of its island components were remote from one another. Geographically and socially it was as diverse as could be imagined. One island might be inhabited by a single family and its retainers, while another was host to a complex and ordered society of chiefs and nobles. Weather conditions varied dramatically: in Hawaii, Polynesians basked in the sun; on the Chatham Islands, off New Zealand, they wrapped themselves in sealskin coats. Yet, for all this disparity, they retained a remarkably homogenous culture centred on the sea that both linked and divided them.

Opposite: **A traditionally carved Maori figure in the Te Hau-Ki-Turanga meeting house of the Ngati Kaipoho people, *c.*1842. The person depicted is Raharuhi Rukopo, the chief who organized the work.**

Polynesians respected diversity, developing vast pantheons of deities, each of which represented some aspect of the environment. To control this profusion they instituted a protocol in which chiefs were not only temporal rulers but, as descendants of the gods, spiritual go-betweens who interceded with the heavens on behalf of their subjects. Working within the constraints of ritual calendars, the chiefs built temples and organized sacrifices and festivals to bring prosperity to the world. They also regulated a complex system of taboos, whereby certain objects or activities were closed to a particular section of society or, in extremity, forbidden to all. These interdictions helped maintain traditional values and the breaking of one could be the cause of any manner of disaster, although the unpredictable hurricanes, earthquakes, tidal waves and volcanic eruptions that plagued the area were more usually traced to quarrels between the gods. The taboos of incest and cannibalism were often employed in mythology to explain humankind's state of imperfection.

The first European visitors saw Polynesia as an unspoiled paradise, a welcoming place where Western taboos regarding sex and material possessions did not exist. It was true that Polynesians generally accepted strangers and had different laws of ownership or sexual exclusivity, but Polynesia was not the placid, moral-free society of Western fantasy. It was rigidly ordered and any deviation from that order was frowned upon. Ironically, it was just such a misunderstanding which brought the area infamy when Captain Cook was murdered – mistaken for a god who had broken the unwritten code.

Above: **Evocative symbol of a lost era and culture, this *moai maea* statue on Easter Island has had its eyes restored and red top-knot replaced. Such stone figures were a key part of the island's ceremonial complexes.**

The Seeds of Life

As a society of seafarers and travellers, Polynesians laid strong emphasis on their origins. Immediately, they looked no farther back than Havaiki, a legendary homeland from which their forbears had first migrated into the Pacific. But beyond that lay a region of darkness and chaos in which the seeds of life had first been sown.

Geographically, Havaiki was a nebulous place. Translating simply as "the place our ancestors came from", it could have been anywhere on the Asian mainland or, more probably, in the Melanesian islands that stretched out towards Polynesia. For some of the later migrants, such as those who settled New Zealand and the Chatham Islands, Havaiki may even have referred to a point in Polynesia itself – possibly Samoa, Tonga, the Marquesas or Tahiti – from which they later dispersed across the ocean. Wherever it lay, however, Havaiki was universally embraced as the wellspring of Polynesian culture.

On one level, Havaiki was a concept that could be explained in recognizable, physical terms. But it also carried deeper connotations, sometimes being referred to as the World Below, a dark, primal zone from which was conjured not only humankind but the whole Earth and everything that lived upon it – the World of Light. As one myth explained, "In Havaiki were the beginnings made of many things that concern this world." It was not, however, a realm that died with creation. Instead it lingered on, a parallel state of existence in which dwelled gods and demi-gods who sometimes surfaced to influence events on the human plane.

Havaiki – or Po, as it was also known – was interpreted in many different ways. To Hawaiians it was a state of chaos that was itself the disorganized ruins of an even earlier world. They could not guess what either place was like, but they evolved a remarkably scientific view of how their environment had come into being. They described a time of darkness in which the first life forms were corals, shellfish and worms. As other creatures made their appearance – among them the octopus, a terrible predator of whom the others lived in fear – the ocean-dwellers fought for survival among themselves. Their dead and decaying corpses fell to the seabed, piling up to such an extent that eventually they rose above the waters to become dry land. A few inhabitants of the sea adapted to the land, in order to escape the octopus. But then the land began to exhibit the characteristics Polynesians knew so well: earthquakes and volcanic eruptions. These served not to destroy, however, but to create. In their aftermath came the first glimmerings of light, followed by the emergence of plants, pigs and mice. At the same time, the sea became filled with

Tamatekapua (top) was the captain of the ship of first people which voyaged from Havaiki. His brother Whakaturia holds a basket of breadfruit the two had stolen on stilts from a chief's garden.

new species – fishes, whales and porpoises – that drove the octopus into the nooks and crannies where it still lives today. From this period of activity were born thought and logical reasoning. Without a vessel to contain it, the new intelligence was nothing but an abstract concept. In the final stages of creation, however, came men, women and gods into whom intelligence was poured. The light brightened to full strength and the teeming, sunlit world of Polynesia came into being.

Not all accounts were so generalized. In the Cook Islands, for example, Havaiki took the form of a six-layered coconut shell at the bottom of which dwelled the Mother-of-All, a spirit woman named Vari-ma-te-takere who brought the world to life. In New Zealand it was an Earth Mother called Papa who gave birth to the gods by whom the world was subsequently created.

Tahitians ascribed creation to a feathered deity named Tangaroa-tahitumu, or "Tangaroa the origin". To them, Havaiki was initially a void in which Tangaroa revolved in the round shell that was his home. After a time he wearied of his confinement and cracked open the shell. He called out to the sky and to the earth, to the rocks and to the sand, but there was no answer. In search of company, he turned over one half of his shell and lifted it up to form the sky. He made the other half into the Earth. Piece by piece, Tangaroa used his own body to give the world features. His backbone became a mountain range and his ribs the ridges running down its sides. His entrails were turned into clouds. The rest of his insides were made into lobsters, shrimps and eels. He used his feathers to make plants and his toenails and fingernails to provide scales and shells for the sea creatures. His blood floated away to give the world colour. Later, as his creation expanded and flourished, Tangaroa peopled it with gods and humans made from the remnants of his flesh. Eventually only his head remained, surviving on its own as a sacred entity to be worshipped by the world's inhabitants.

A Divine Colour

In a world dominated by just three colours – the blue of the sea and sky, the white of the sand and clouds, the green of the trees – Polynesians revered the colour red, with its connotations of blood and life.

On most islands, the commonest source of red was the plumage of tropical birds. Elsewhere it was dragged from the ground in the form of red clay or rock. In Tahiti the colour had divine origins; it was the blood of the creator god Tangaroa, which coloured everything from sunsets to rainbows. Throughout Polynesia, red was associated with divinity and scarlet feathers were plucked from a variety of birds to fashion capes that were worn as symbols of royal authority. Captain Cook related that red feathers – plucked from the head of a tiny bird, the vini – were to Tahitians "as valuable as jewels are in Europe". Where red birds were scarce, the islanders used other materials. In New Zealand, red ochre was mixed with shark's blood and daubed on sacred objects. In the statue-building society of Easter Island, giant stone effigies were given a respectful top-knot of red limestone.

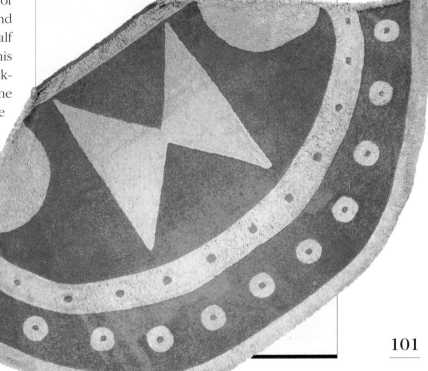

Ingredients of the Universe

To many Polynesians creation was a grand, cosmic event brought about by supernatural forces. But some islanders described it in more intimate terms, using relatively humble images derived from their immediate surroundings.

In the beginning was a spider – or so, at least, some Polynesian myths stated. Spinning webs of extraordinary strength and complexity, the spider was an ideal creator. At the same time it represented death, its corpse-filled web reflecting the natural fate of all living things.

According to the islanders of Nauru there was darkness at the dawn of creation. Through this gloom moved Areop-Enap – Old Spider – searching for food. On one of her forages she discovered a clam. But before she could kill it the clam opened wide, devoured her, and then snapped shut. Dismayed and still hungry, she roamed the clam's insides looking for a way out. In one corner she found a tiny snail. Rather than eat it, which was her first thought, she begged its assistance. If the snail could crawl to the hinge of the clam's shell, she suggested, it might be able to prise open their prison. Off crept the snail over the clam's body, leaving behind it a phosphorescent trail. In its light, Areop-Enap saw that they were not alone: there was a third captive, a white worm called Rigi. While the snail went about its task, Areop-Enap cast a spell of strength on Rigi and ordered him to break open the shell.

Rigi braced himself between the two halves of the shell and pushed. Time and again he shoved, but the shell remained closed. He strained until the sweat poured down his body. It

This Society Islands' mourning dress makes significant use of pearl shell, turtleshell plaques and coconut shell. The mask is bound with braided human hair, a reminder of the unbroken chain of ancestors who gave the social elite their *mana*.

Sky and Moon

Polynesians viewed the night sky as a heavenly manifestation of tapa, *the white cloth that their women made by beating bark to a pulp. The stars were* tapa *visible as uncovered holes in a dark celestial blanket through which the winds blew until they were blocked by a divine thumb. As for the moon, it was home to the goddess Hina.*

In Tahitian legend, Hina was the wife of the god Tangaroa. Every night she would beat *tapa* for her husband. The noise irritated Tangaroa tremendously, and he asked his fellow god Pani to tell Hina to stop. Hina refused to stop. Pani reported this to Tangaroa who was very annoyed. "Go to her again," he told Pani, "and make her stop. The harbour of the god is noisy."

Pani repeated this message to Hina. It had no effect. He delivered it a third time. Still Hina kept beating the *tapa*. At that, Pani was so furious that he seized Hina's *tapa* mallet and cracked open her skull.

Hina died. But her spirit flew to the moon, where she continued her *tapa* beating. The result of her relentless labours, waxing and waning, remained visible for Tangaroa and all others to see.

ran off him in rivers, creating first a pool, then a lake and finally an entire sea. It was this, rather than Rigi's strength, that was the clam's undoing. The saltwater killed it and its shell sprang open.

Areop-Enap made the lower shell, with its in-built sea, into the Earth. She made islands from lumps of the clam's flesh and wove each one a covering of vegetation. From the top half of the shell she made the sky and placed the snail on it to become the moon. But then, when she turned to Rigi, she found him dead, drowned in the sea of his own sweat. She wrapped him in a cocoon of silk and set him in the sky – the Milky Way.

In Kiribati, myths say that the world came about thanks to Nareau, or Lord Spider. This being had two separate characters: Old Nareau made the gods, moulding them out of wet sand, while Young Nareau undertook the task of making the universe and all the creatures that lived within it.

In the absence of suitable building materials, Young Nareau was forced to use the gods created by Old Nareau. He killed and dismembered Na Atibu, the first god to have been formed, setting his right eye in the sky as the sun and his left as the moon. Na Atibu's brains became clouds, his bones islands and his flesh the plants that covered them. His fleas, meanwhile, were transformed into beasts and humans.

Young Nareau having assembled the ingredients of the universe, it was left to Na Kika, the octopus god, to set them in their proper places with his tentacles. But there was one problem: Na Atibu's brains were too heavy. Unable to hang in the air they sank down onto the land, bringing the sky with them. Young Nareau sought the help of Riiki, an eel, who slid between Earth and sky and pushed them apart, holding up Na Atibu's brains until they were used to their new home.

Rangi and Papa, Creators Supreme

The Maori peoples evolved the concept of two supreme creator beings from whom sprang an orderly pantheon of gods, each with his or her own sphere of responsibility. The gods controlled the sea, the weather, the trees, the fish, the animals and every other aspect of life. They also gave birth to humans and ordered the conditions in which they lived.

According to Maori myth, life began with a perfect and absolute void. It was not mere darkness – in itself a source of horror – but something worse, a state of utter emptiness devoid of light, feeling and form. The term used to describe it was *kore*, an expression that later worked its way into the Maori calendar, being used to mark the three nights in each lunar month during which it was supposed to be impossible to obtain food from either land or sea.

Into this state of nothingness emerged two beings, Rangi the sky god and Papa the Earth goddess. They owed their existence to a shadowy parent deity called Io, a name that would later delight Christian missionaries who linked it to Jehovah. Clasped together like a shell, Rangi and Papa produced six children, Tane god of forests, Tangaroa god of the sea, Tu god of war, Rongo god of cultivated plants, Haumia god of wild plants and Tawhiri god of the elements. The space between Rangi and Papa was hot and fecund, giving birth

A *pare* or door lintel for a meeting house from the Bay of Plenty, *c.*1840. The three male figures represent Tane and two of his brother gods pushing apart their primal parents, Rangi and Papa.

to trees, ferns, lizards and shellfish. But it was also dark and cramped. Unable to stand, the gods crawled around blindly like lizards, or simply lay on their sides, struggling for breath.

Then a miraculous thing happened. Papa raised her arm and the children caught a brief glimpse of daylight. Immediately they wanted more. Tane suggested they separate their parents, a move which was greeted enthusiastically by all except Tawhiri, who was very attached to his father the sky. But they soon found that speech was easier than action. One by one they struggled to prise the Earth and sky apart. Their efforts were to no avail until Tu had the idea of cutting through Rangi's arms which were clasped tight around Papa. This did the trick and by standing on his head and bracing his feet against the sky Tane was able to split his parents' embrace. With the help of his brothers, Tane used wooden poles to support Rangi in his new position. Forever afterwards Rangi and Papa were immutably divided, expressing their grief with tears that fell as rain from the sky and mists that rose at dawn from the Earth.

Tu's violence not only allowed the Earth and sky to be separated but also gave the world the gift of blood. In many Polynesian myths, blood was an essential part of creation, providing the red hues that islanders associated with kingship and virility. In Tahiti the blood was supplied by Tangaroa, a lesser god in the Maori pantheon who had been elevated there to the status of creator. In Maori stories the blood came from the amputation of Rangi's arms. Falling to the ground, it coloured the earth red, creating the ochre with which people and religious objects were daubed.

Tane's prowess made him one of the predominant gods in the pantheon. He was credited with creating light, in the shape of the sun and the moon, and with clothing his father with stars to hide his dark nakedness. In some legends he was also hailed as the first planter of trees, an experiment that was not successful initially. Tane modelled his forestry along human lines, with the trees' legs, or branches, being embedded in the ground while their roots waved in the air like hair. Then, realizing that something was wrong, he reversed them to emulate his own stance when he had divided the Earth and sky. The trees' hair took root and soon they were providing food for birds, animals and humans.

Tane's success at separating his parents led to tempestuous sibling rivalry. A jealous Tawhiri blew down Tane's forests, causing the fish that had previously lived on dry land to flee to the ocean. This in turn caused an everlasting feud between Tane and Tangaroa. Tane supplied the trees with which men made canoes to tame the ocean. In retaliation, Tangaroa launched tidal waves that swept away the forests. It was a cycle of revenge that neatly explained the main elements of Polynesian existence.

Tane was promiscuous, mating with a variety of beings to produce animals, stones and grass. Then, on Rangi's advice, he sculpted a human woman and mated with her. Hine-titama, or Dawn Maiden, was born and Tane slept with her too. When Hine discovered who her father was she was horrified. She fled to the underworld, and vowed to drag all Tane's children down after her. Undeterred, Tane next produced the ancestors of all humankind. But Tane's children could never be immortal like their father. Inexorably they were pulled to their graves by his vengeful daughter.

Tane Mahutia is New Zealand's largest kauri tree, named after Tane, god of the forests. A tall, straight hardwood, it forms a living link between Earth and sky.

The Quarrelsome Elements

After the beginning came the gods, often seen as different personifications of an overall divine force. They were the stars, the winds, the seas and all other natural forces that were beyond human reckoning. Initially, however, they were quarrelsome and it took a series of major conflicts before the Polynesian universe settled into an orderly rhythm.

In New Zealand, and some other parts of the region, these strife myths told of the god Tane, the embodiment of light and wisdom, who sought to bring the gift of knowledge to humans. Set against him was Whiro, the god of darkness and evil.

Knowledge was contained within three baskets belonging to Io. In one basket was the knowledge of peace and love, in another the knowledge of prayers and religious ritual, and in the third was the knowledge of survival and war. Io invited Tane to deliver the baskets to the World of Light. In accordance with Io's wishes, Tane scattered their contents across Polynesia, erecting temples to act as repositories for the sacred gift. Jealous that Tane had been chosen for the task, Whiro did his best to stop him. He sent hordes of centipedes, spiders, moths and ants to attack Tane. The two sides met in a mighty battle from which Tane emerged victorious. But although Whiro's forces were defeated they could not be crushed, and their descendants remained on Earth to plague humankind. Whiro, similarly, could not be killed. He was driven to the underworld, from where he dispensed a destructive legacy of sickness, evil thoughts and death.

The moral of every conflict lay in its aftermath. Against the baleful influence of Whiro could be set Tane's gift of knowledge and the institution of temples that gave men contact with the gods.

On the archipelago of Tuamotu the main protagonists were thought to be Tane and Atea, two gods who inhabited different layers of Heaven. As the two battled for supremacy, Tane saw that he was losing and slipped through the layers to seek temporary refuge on Earth.

Tane enjoyed his time among humans and even acquired a taste for cooked food. This was an important change: Polynesians believed that the gods derived sustenance from raw materials and that cooked, spiritless food was anathema.

Tiring of his exile, Tane made his way back to Heaven. To his horror he found that most of his family had either been killed by Atea or had fled. All that remained were his father and a number of ancient ancestors. Worse still, Heaven did not contain the food to which he had grown accustomed.

Tane was still determined to overcome Atea so he visited the thunder god, Fatutiri, and obtained the gift of lightning. His father warned him not to use it at once; better, he counselled, to wait until Atea was old and weak. In due course, when his father's hair had become silver, Tane,

backed by a band of heavenly allies, met Atea in a duel to determine who was the strongest. The test was to be the power of making fire. Atea rubbed sticks together and produced a flame but Tane blew it out. They changed places and this time Atea tried to blow out Tane's flame. But thanks to Tane's gift of lightning the fire refused to be extinguished. In fact, ironically, the more Atea blew on it the stronger it became.

While the contest was underway one of Tane's followers became jealous of his power and stole a light with which he set fire to the heavens themselves. Tane flew upwards to extinguish it, then returned to delivered the coup de grace to Atea, shooting out a lightning bolt that struck him dead. Then, in recognition of his rival's divinity, Tane set Atea's spirit free on a canoe to float across the southern seas. It came to rest on Tuamotu where it gave rise to a long line of chiefs.

Otago, in South Island, is home to the tallest mountains in Aotearoa ("Land of the Long White Cloud"), and a place where the elemental powers of nature can be appreciated fully.

First Man Tiki

In some Maori myths humankind was brought into the world by Tane. In others, however, it was Tu, the god of war, who created Tiki, the first man. Tiki's children married both gods and mortals, begetting a chain of descent that led to the royal lineages of Aotearoa (New Zealand).

Tu provided the means whereby humans could survive. He also devised a way in which they could multiply. Seeing how Tane had created a woman from sand, Tu moulded a similar model and breathed life into it. But there were two crucial difference between his and Tane's creation: Tu's model was of a man, not a woman; and it was created not from sand but from powerful red ochre. The result was Tiki, who epitomized procreative power and male sexuality. At the same time Tiki was a trickster, combining various beneficial qualities with an irresistible urge to throw society into disarray.

Tiki himself later made a model of a woman, just as the god Tane had done, and produced a daughter, Tiaki, the first in a line of humans. The concept of Tiki was widespread throughout Polynesia, carrying connotations of power and virility, as well as providing the necessary genealogical link between human rulers and their divine ancestors. The manner in which Tiki and his wife were moulded from earth also reflected the way in which many Polynesians created their own environment. On their travels they often had to ferry cargoes of earth from one island to another to enrich the thin soil. Thus, in reality as in myth, life was moulded out of soil.

Tiki, creator of all children, was the link between humankind and the divine ancestors; carved human figures were called *tiki*. This 19th-century detail from a meeting house's central post represents an ancestor of the tribe that owned the house.

As the first man, Tiki's life bore striking resemblances to that of Tane, the predominant god. His wife was called Hina-one, or Earth Maiden, and she, like Tane's daughter Hine-titama, fled to the underworld after a quarrel with Tiki. Just as Tane slept with his own daughter so, too, did Tiki, causing her to seek refuge with her mother below. So close was the connection that the tales of Tiki and Tane occasionally mingled, with Tiki being portrayed as the son of Tane, or as the husband of Tane's granddaughter.

Unlike Tane, however, Tiki was viewed as a somewhat scurrilous trickster. His voracious sexual appetite was reflected in the name borne by the Maoris' famous *hei-tiki* fertility symbols. In this regard, his behaviour went well beyond all the bounds of decency or social convention. On one occasion he supposedly persuaded his own daughter Tiaki to sleep with him by pretending to be a different person who happened by chance to look like her father. The ruse worked horribly well, earning for Tiki the epithet of *kaikaia*, a title that implied both incest and cannibalism.

Tiki, it was said, could assume two faces. One was so handsome that all women fell in love with him. The other was so disgusting that women wanted to kill him on sight. Rumour had it that he kept his ugly features hidden inside his body, wearing them when the mood came upon him. He was also seemingly indestructible. Once, when Tiki put on his ugly face, the people caught him. They tried to pull out his eyes but without success. The same thing happened when they tried to remove his teeth. They tied his tongue in a knot but the knot untied itself. They cut off his ears, feet, arms and penis but Tiki simply stuck them back on. Finally they sliced him open and unravelled his intestines across the ground. At this indignity Tiki fled in tears and hid under the sand until his pride was restored.

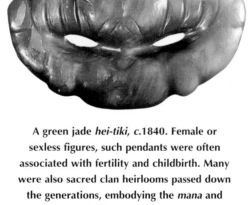

A green jade *hei-tiki, c.*1840. Female or sexless figures, such pendants were often associated with fertility and childbirth. Many were also sacred clan heirlooms passed down the generations, embodying the *mana* and prestige of the family's links to the gods.

This tale was repeated in many forms. Sometimes narrative tension was heightened by Tiki changing in mid-torture to his beautiful form and then reverting to ugliness once he had been released. Typically, he sought refuge in the sand after surviving prolonged and unsuccessful attempts to destroy him.

In one version his end came while he was recovering in the sand. As he was lying there, with just his eyes showing, an eel seized his heel. He called to his wife to help him but she was reluctant. "I am tired of sleeping with a demon," she said. Nevertheless, she took his head and began a tug-of-war with the eel who was pulling on Tiki's foot. The strain grew greater and greater and then, in mid-contest, Tiki suddenly disappeared.

Perhaps as punishment for his misdemeanours, Tiki was denied the gift of immortality. But he lived on in artistic form, his name being given to the images that Maoris carved from wood and greenstone to represent their ancestors. In this guise he usually appeared with bird-like features – three-taloned hands, ear tufts, slanting eyes and a beaked face – that brought to mind an owl. The likeness was no coincidence, for the owl was associated with Rua, a hero who had won the secret of carving from the gods. Fittingly, the first man was linked to the origins of his portrayal.

A Dynasty of Nobles

To fill the ancestral gap between themselves and Tiki, the first man, the Maoris invented a host of human heroes. One of them was Rua with his divine gift of carving (see page 112); another was Mataora, who introduced tattooing (see pages 112–113). But the best known heroes were Tawhaki and Rata, whose exploits gave rise to a noble dynasty.

The Tawhaki Cycle comprised the saga of a single family and was popular not only in New Zealand but in most of Polynesia's outlying islands. Passing through the generations, it told of humiliation and revenge, of battles with gods and man, and of a final triumphant sea voyage to establish a community in a new land. Outwardly a tale of heroism, it reflected with startling accuracy the last phase of Polynesian migration in which families dispersed from the central islands to avoid internecine warfare and overcrowding.

The main hero was Tawhaki, a man whose fair hair, golden-red skin and irresistible sex appeal immediately identified him with divinity. He did, in fact, have divine blood being the grandson of Whatiri, a thunder-goddess from whom he inherited the ability to cast lightning bolts from his armpits. On the human side, Tawhaki's family tree was less illustrious. His grandfather, Kai-tangata, was a cannibal who met his end when a latrine collapsed on his head during a visit to the underworld. His father, Hema, meanwhile was so filthy as a child that Whatiri, Hema's mother, deserted her family in disgust. Later, Hema quarrelled with the gods and was imprisoned in an underworld cesspit.

Tawhaki and his brother Karihi determined to rescue Hema. Kahiri, however, was a poor choice of companion. Whereas Tawhaki excelled at everything to such an extent that he was cordially disliked by his fellows, Kahiri was an over-eager incompetent. It was only through Tawhaki's skill and his knowledge of the correct spells needed to visit the underworld that the two of them survived the trip and successfully rescued their father.

Tawhaki's downfall came when jealous men stripped his golden skin as he slept and threw it into the sea to be devoured by fishes. Now ordinary looking, he no longer attracted women. Eventually he used his divine connections to regain his skin – only one portion was unobtainable, that which covered the soles of his feet – and once more he was an object of desire. But he was full of bitterness at his earlier rejection, and left his homeland to seek a better place.

The epic continued with Rata, Tawhaki's grandson. Like Tawhaki, Rata sought to avenge his father, who had been devoured by a bird-god named Matuku-takotako. At the same time he sought to rescue his mother who had been stolen by Matuku and planted head-down with her feet in the air to act as a food stand for the gods. Unlike Tawhaki, Rata had no divine powers. Although brave and resourceful he was untutored in magic spells. His main skill lay in the construction of war canoes. Fortunately, the underworld in which his mother was captive had risen to the surface and taken the shape of an island. Sailing towards it with a crew of select warriors, Rata battled his way past sea demons and succeeded in defeating the gods who held his mother captive. He also managed to retrieve his father's head from the gullet of Matuku. Rata later married the daughter of a god and their union produced a line from which all later rulers were descended.

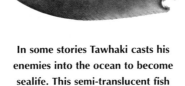

In some stories Tawhaki casts his enemies into the ocean to become sealife. This semi-translucent fish amulet is from Ruapuke Island.

Hina, the Eel and the Coconut

Hina (translating simply as "young woman") was seen as the divinity of women and women's work. She appeared in different guises throughout Polynesian mythology. In a culture where the composition of love poems and the initiation of courtship were the exclusive province of women, some of Hina's tales were blatantly sexual and others practical.

Hina's favourite bathing spot was a deep, dark sea pool that was full of eels. Normally they fled at her approach, but one eel was larger and more daring than the rest. As Hina relaxed in the water the eel wound itself around her legs. Hina did not discourage it. In fact she let it approach her whenever she went into the pool.

One day, as she was gazing at the eel, it transformed into a handsome young man called Tuna. They became lovers. But Tuna always changed back to an eel after every visit so that nobody would suspect their liaison. Finally, Tuna brought the affair to a close. He announced that a great rain would come, causing a flood that would rise to the door of Hina's house. But she was not to be afraid, for Tuna would swim up to her home and lay his head on the threshold. She was then to cut off his head, bury it on some high ground and see what happened next.

Everything occurred as Tuna had predicted, and Hina duly cut off his head and buried it. The waters subsided and all was normal again. Where the head had been interred, however, two green shoots appeared. The shoots flourished and grew into coconut trees that provided humankind with milk, flesh and oil, with leaves for baskets, with shells for bowls, with fibre for ropes and with trunks that could be made into house pillars and canoes. Lest people forget their benefactor all they had to do was remove the husk of a ripened coconut: there they would find markings of the two small eyes and mouth of an eel.

Artistry in Wood and Flesh

Many Maori myths told of the acquisition by humans of vital skills, foodstuffs and materials from the underworld. The hard jadeite that was used to make axes came from the gods, as did staples such as the sweet potato. The skills of weaving and bird-snaring likewise had divine origins, and so did the highly recognizable styles evident in Maori carving and tattooing.

Artistically, one of the most striking features of Maori society was the elaborate carving that decorated wooden objects ranging from canoe prows to roof supports. Unique to New Zealand, thanks to the quality of its timber and its plentiful deposits of steel-hard jadeite that could be made into adzes and axes, the skill of carving was said to have been stolen from the gods by a folk hero named Rua.

Its introduction to the human world came about when Tangaroa, god of the ocean, snatched Rua's son and took him down to the seabed. On hearing what had happened, Rua immediately dived into the ocean and swam down to Tangaroa's house. He found himself in an extraordinary place. Not only was his son pinned to the gable as a decoration, but the house was full of carvings so lifelike that some of them could even talk. Before he could rescue his son, however, Rua had to destroy Tangaroa's followers, the predatory fish who fed at night before returning to Tangaroa's home to rest. Knowing that the fish could not survive in sunlight, he blocked every crevice he could see with mud and waited. The next day he set fire to the house while the fish were still asleep. In the absence of sunlight the fish thought it was night and fled out the door, only to perish in the sun's rays. Rua collected his son safely, and before returning to the world above he plucked a few carved pillars from Tangaroa's burning home. From these mementoes sprang the art of Maori carving.

Maori tattoos, whose curling designs closely resembled those of their carvings, had a similar genesis. According to legend, they were brought to the world by Mataora, a human who had married a goddess. Unfortunately, he made the mistake of beating his wife, who then fled to the underworld in disgust. Full of remorse, Mataora went after her. Journeying through the underworld he came across the god Uetonga, tapping a tattoo into a fellow god's face. Surprised, Mataora pointed to his own facial decorations which had been painted on with ochre, and informed Uetonga that he was going about things in the wrong way. Uetonga merely laughed, and to show his opinion of such a transitory cosmetic he reached out and smeared Mataora's ochre into messy blotches. Mataora accordingly had his face tattooed. It was a painful experience. Indeed, when he eventually found his wife his face was so swollen that he could hardly see. But the pain was worthwhile: Mataora's wife admired his courage; and when the swelling subsided she found him so handsome that she agreed to return to the upper world.

A unique sculpture which represents Tangaroa, creator and sea god of Polynesia, a divine figure so huge he breathes only twice a day – what humans call the tides. This 17th- or 18th-century carving from Rurutu in the Austral Islands depicts him in the act of creating the other gods and people, seen all over his face and body. The statue has a lidded opening at the back into which smaller objects can be placed. Such a work resonates with *tapu*.

When he left the underworld, however, Mataora made a fatal mistake. As a parting gift, Uetonga had given him a woven cloak, a thing unknown to humans. In addition, Mataora had collected three new species – the owl, the bat and the kiwi – to take home. Upon reaching the gate to the underworld its guardian asked what he was carrying with him. He declared everything save the cloak, which had slipped his memory. Already disgusted at Mataora's wife-beating, the guardian was further outraged at this apparent deception. He let Mataora pass, but vowed that never again would a human leave the home of the gods.

Thus Mataora, whose name means Face of Vitality, brought the art of tattooing and weaving to humankind. He also filled the Aotearoan night with life – for the owl, the bat and the kiwi only come out in the dark. But he closed the portals to the underworld. From that time on, no living person would return from its depths.

The Power and Mystique of *Waka*

Canoes played a vital part in Maori life. They were all-important for sea travel, for fishing and for warfare. They were also revered as the means whereby Polynesian culture first reached New Zealand.

On their migrations the Polynesians employed double-hulled, wind-powered catamaran canoes, or *waka*, unique to the Pacific. Sea-going marvels that were constructed without a single piece of iron, these vessels carried the Maoris to their home. Each canoe had a name – Tainui, Te Arawa, Aotea, Tokomaru, Takitimu, Kurahaupo and Matatua – and their human cargoes later formed tribes named after the craft on which they had first arrived.

Whether used as catamarans for long-distance travel, as sleek single-hulled war boats, or as simple fishing vessels, canoes were surrounded by mystique.

It was impossible, for example, for men to cook food on a canoe. Women, to whom the taboo did not apply, had to accompany the fleet and ferry meals to their husbands and sons. It was the women's job too to compose the chants to which warriors kept time as they paddled across the waves.

The elaborately carved prows and stern-posts of canoes were their owners' pride. When a chief died his memorial would often be the hull of his canoe set upright in the ground and bearing his stylized image.

A model of a war canoe, *c.* 1850, at one time the most decorated and highly prized of clan possessions.

113

The Annual Cycle of Ku and Lono

One of the largest and most sophisticated of Polynesian societies, Hawaii, like New Zealand, had its own particular culture. Central to its identity was the ritual cycle through which the gods were propitiated and the authority of the chiefs enhanced.

Dominating the Hawaiian calendar were two gods, Ku and Lono, whose good favour was essential to humankind's well-being. Their spheres of influence were clearly marked by the weather. The rainy season was the period of Lono (known elsewhere as Rongo), the god of the sky, peace and cultivation. The rest of the year was dominated by Ku (called Tu on other islands) who was the god of the earth and warfare, and also associated with fishing, canoe building and magic. In the rites conducted during his ascendancy Ku came close to personifying all the attributes of humankind, thus emphasizing the divine connections enjoyed by Hawaii's rulers.

Ensuring the orderly continuation of this cycle was all-important. Any disruption would be fatal to Hawaiian agriculture. It would also shatter the balance of earthly power, for the chiefs who controlled the cult of Lono were also held responsible for the island's fertility. Should the food supply fail it would be seen as a sure sign of the chiefs' political impotence.

The advent of Lono was marked when the Pleiades constellation became visible in the evening sky. This was the signal for the four-month-long festival of Makihiki to begin. The first part of the festival comprised a lengthy procession during which

A late 18th-century wooden figure of Ku, Hawaiian creator and war god, one of the local trinity, with Kane and Lono, which created man and the universe. Man was made in the image of Kane, shaped by Ku and breathed into life by all three.

A Tragic Case of Mistaken Identity

The murder of Captain James Cook, the first European to visit Hawaii, may well have been caused by his inadvertent arrival during the festival of Makihiki.

The death of Captain Cook, stabbed with the iron daggers from Birmingham he brought as gifts, by J. Cleveley.

Cook landed on Hawaii in November 1778, just as the Makihiki was about to begin, and after a brief stay sailed off clockwise around the island. Assuming that this year Lono had decided to appear in person – throughout Polynesia pale skin was associated with divinity – the Hawaiians jubilantly awaited Cook's return. Sure enough, he did make another stop on the island, whereupon he was taken to the temple of Lono and invited to participate in the ritual responses. Imagining that he was merely being taught their language, Cook went along with his hosts' request. Then, in an

unfortunate coincidence, he announced his departure precisely at the time when Lono was due to leave the island for his home in Kahiki. All might have gone well had Cook not then had to repair one of his ships. He returned to Hawaii on 11 February 1779 to the bewilderment of its inhabitants. The chiefs were worried and angry; either he was another Paao, and a threat to them, or he was an undead Lono and misfortune would follow – either way their authority would be undermined. They took matters into their own hands, and killed him in the surf.

the image of Lono was carried clockwise around Hawaii and its nearby islands – any other direction would have augured badly for the Hawaiian king's authority – to the accompaniment of singing, dancing, wrestling matches and displays of athletic prowess. At regular intervals its progress was punctuated to make sure Lono was well fed. The local chiefs conducted sacrifices to curry the god's favour, and their wives offered gifts of food in the hope that they would be blessed with children.

Whereas the Makihiki was said to have been instituted by Lono himself, its sacrificial rites were laid at the door of Paao, a god who had come from invisible islands across the sea to install a new religion and a new royal lineage in Hawaii. The connection reflected a widespread belief that Hawaii's rulers were foreigners who had overthrown the original dynasty – a reasonably accurate account of migration that was echoed throughout Polynesia.

When the circuit of the islands was complete, the Makihiki entered its final phase. The effigy was brought ashore and installed in a temple dedicated to Lono. Here, to the accompaniment of chants and responses, the god was defeated in a ritual battle with Ku and left Hawaii for his home in the invisible land of Kahiki – another name for Tahiti. From then on, Ku was in the ascendancy and Lono would not return until the following winter when the Pleiades reappeared on the horizon, bringing in their wake the life-giving rains.

For centuries, the placatory rituals were conducted without major incident. They were disrupted in November 1778, however, when James Cook landed on Hawaii. His arrival coincided with the Makihiki and caused a degree of fear and confusion that climaxed in his murder. Whatever the reason for Cook's death, the explorer's coming had grave repercussions. To a degree it brought about the calamity it was intended to avert.

Powers to Destroy and Powers to Heal

Hawaii was unique in many ways. Not only was it situated in the northern hemisphere – the rest of Polynesia lay below the equator – but it was dominated by the world's largest live volcano. This inescapable, lava-spewing presence inevitably found its way into island mythology, being identified as the goddess Pele. She assumed such a dominant position in the pantheon that she was credited with the creation of the whole Hawaiian Archipelago.

Just as the Hawaiians had emigrated from central Polynesia, so too had their gods journeyed from a homeland in the south – widely assumed to be Tahiti. Leading them was Pele, a goddess who had been driven away for stealing her sister's husband. On reaching Hawaii Pele discovered not an island but a massive block of land. Fortunately, her mother had given her an ocean as a parting gift. Pele unleashed the water which poured over the land until only isolated mountaintops could be seen above the waves. The waters later ebbed, leaving a chain of islands dotted across the sea.

Up to then, Pele had not found her true vocation in life. Thinking that she might be a goddess of water, she roamed the islands digging holes in search of springs. Every attempt was without success, until she began work on the largest island, Hawaii. Here, to her delight and astonishment, her efforts resulted in a gush of lava. Realizing that fire was her true element, she became the goddess of the volcano – Pele the destroyer.

Pele sometimes assumed human form and wandered among the people who dwelled in the shadow of her crater. She was, however, a jealous goddess and her visits often resulted in an eruption. On one occasion, for example, she took a human lover named Lohiau and then deserted him. Lohiau died of a broken heart, at which Pele began to have regrets. She dispatched her sister Hi'iaka to resurrect him and bring him back to her. Hi'iaka did as she was bidden. But she was away so long that Pele assumed she was having an affair with Lohiau and on their return showered them with lava and fiery rocks. One rock killed Lohiau instantly. Being a goddess, however, Hi'iaka could withstand her sister's rage. She snatched up Lohiau's body and took him with her to the underworld, where they lived as man and wife. As Pele became older she became more forgetful, but sometimes the memory of her imagined wrong would return and then, as her anger boiled over, rivers of lava turned Hawaii into a blackened ruin.

Pele's fury could be roused by a number of things. When no obvious explanation presented

The vast majority of the world's active volcanoes are found in the Pacific region. Brimful of passion, Pele, goddess of fire and the Kilauea Volcano, must never be crossed, for her wrath can erupt in a river of lava and an explosion of red hot rock.

Teaching the Ancient Wisdom

The transmission of Polynesian lore was not left to chance but was institutionalized in a sophisticated educational system. In the central and eastern regions almost every island had its own school or intellectual establishment that disseminated ancient wisdoms.

The Society Islands boasted a number of colleges where *tahu'a*, or priestly teachers, instructed male and female pupils in everything from religion and poetic composition to medicine and canoe building. The teachers – whose name meant "Cave of many outlets" – were usually drawn from the families of priests and had to undergo a strict training programme before being allowed to practise. A period of education in esoteric studies was followed by a retreat in which they communed with the gods and finally by an oral examination before a group of elders. Successful applicants were honoured with a feast before taking their place in the schools. One island, Opoa, became such a centre of religious learning that it drew European comparisons with Mecca and Rome – as well as the less complimentary epithet, "the metropolis of idolatry". So powerful was the influence wielded by Opoa's seminary that it was able to twist myth to suit politics. Tangaroa, who was elsewhere merely a god, became a creator deity in the Society Islands probably because a powerful Tahitian chief claimed him as an ancestor.

Not everywhere was as advanced as the Society Islands. But most places had some form of school or, at the least, a body of experts who kept the flame of knowledge burning. Intellectual games and contests that promoted the skills of poetry, narration and chanting were widespread. In Hawaii, the royal courts sponsored competitions to refine the allusions and similes that were the essence of oral tradition. Those of high birth were expected to excel in this area, but it was not a closed shop; recognition was awarded to anyone who possessed the necessary talent.

The intellectual process reached its apogee not in Polynesia's heartland but, ironically, in its farthest outpost – Easter Island. Here the teachers developed a script called *rongorongo*. Restricted to a college of priests, the sacred writing was inscribed on wooden "talking boards" that were deployed at important ceremonies. Not as yet fully deciphered, it comprised some 120 basic symbols that could be combined to make between 1,500 and 2,000 ideograms, many of which had multiple meanings. Designed primarily to record ritual and historical traditions, *rongorongo* was written on perishable materials such as cloth or bark and little evidence of its existence remains. There is even a suspicion that it was a post-colonial phenomenon.

During Austral Islands' gatherings in the sacred *marae* to transmit lore, this small stone deity held centre stage.

117

itself, the breaking of a taboo was used as a cautionary explanation for her behaviour. Usually, however, the objects of her rage managed to escape to another island, where they waited until her ardour had cooled before returning.

As befitted a nation of dwellers by the sea, Hawaiians envisaged Pele as a fiery surfer who balanced on the lava crests as they rolled down the slopes. Her manifestation was mimicked by a risky sled contest called *papa holua*. Performed during the festival of Makihiki, it involved men hurling themselves down the mountainside on oiled sleds. Whoever travelled farthest was the winner. It was a dangerous sport that could end in broken bones, if not death. Given her jealous nature it was not surprising that Pele should have wanted to excel at *papa holua*. One year, therefore, she assumed human form and challenged a well-known champion called Kahawali to a race. The result was

foregone. Pele was not only unskilled, but had broken a taboo that forbade women even to touch a *papa holua* sled, let alone take part in a race. When she lost, she exploded in anger. All Kahawali's family died in the lava flow, but he himself escaped in a canoe and, dodging the rocks that Pele hurled at him, made his way to safety.

Lonopuha the Healer

Apart from its volcano, Hawaii embraced a number of other tales particular to itself. One was the narrative of Lonopuha who brought the art of healing to the island. Lonopuha's tale mingled myth – in the shape of Milu, a deity who was said to have ruled Hawaii before becoming king of the underworld – with the factual arrival of an epidemic from other islands. When Milu ruled Hawaii, a group of gods came to the island from Kahiki.

The Cloak, Alu Hula

Cloaks made of red feathers epitomized majesty on Hawaii. They were believed to descend from Alu Hula, the first such garment to be brought to the Hawaiian Archipelago.

The chief of Maui employed runners to carry his messages across the island. The fastest was a man named Eleio of whom it was said that he could run around Maui in the time it took to cook one side of a fish. Eleio also had the gifts of seeing otherwise invisible spirits and returning life to a corpse.

Eleio's job was not always easy. His chief threatened him with death if he was late, and sometimes he would be taunted by spirit women who sought to delay him. When that happened

he would call upon his sister to shame them with a display of her naked bottom. Once, however, Eleio came across a spirit so beautiful that he had to chase her. She ran as fast as he did but he finally caught her at the entrance to a cave. In return for her life she pointed out her parents' home and agreed to bring him their cloak of red feathers, Alu Hula. Hardly had she pledged her word than she disappeared.

They brought with them a sickness that caused headaches, shivering, fever and, ultimately, death. Luckily, they were followed by a man named Kapaka who cured the god Lono of a swollen foot. Lono thereafter assumed a different god-form known as Lonopuha, "Lono of the swollen foot", – although it was swollen only because Lono had driven a digging stick through it while emphasizing to Kapaka that he was not ill – and Kapaka instructed him in the art of herbal healing.

Milu himself fell ill, and when he heard that Lonopuha could heal he sent for him at once. Eschewing herbalism, Lonopuha advised Milu that the best course of action was to stay in bed. So long as he did not get up he would be cured. Milu did as he was told until, after twenty days, he heard a great commotion. A beautiful bird had been seen flying through the sky. Milu could not resist the temptation. He left his sickbed to see what was happening. The bird swooped down and, worming its beak through Milu's armpit, plucked out his liver.

Lonopuha pursued the bird to its lair and by collecting Milu's blood, which was splattered across a nearby stone, he was able to save the king's life. But he warned Milu that his convalescence would succeed only if he stayed in bed. He was not to get up even if he heard the cheers of the annual surf-riding competition. Once again, Milu ignored medical advice. On hearing the shouts of the surfers he could not help going out to join the contest. For two rides he was the darling of the crowds. But on his third he hit the sand awkwardly and was drawn out by the undertow.

Lonopuha continued his healing but Milu was never seen again. His end was summarized tersely: "This concludes the story of Milu's disobedience in this world. Afterwards he was below."

Disgruntled, Eleio went to find the cloak himself. He met the spirit woman's parents and made a deal: he would restore their daughter to life in return for the cloak. This time the bargain was honoured. Eleio was given not only the cloak but the spirit-woman as a wife. Yet there was one big problem: Eleio was late.

He worked his way past the sentries and presented his master with two gifts: the first was a beautiful wife – the resurrected spirit-woman – and the second was Alu Hula. The chief accepted the offerings and spared Eleio. From that time Hawaiian royalty wore a cloak of red feathers and boasted their descent from the spirit world.

Springboard to the Eastern Pacific

Western Polynesia, which incorporated Tonga and Samoa, was the springboard from which Polynesian culture was launched across the Pacific. Both geographically and mythologically, it was closer to Melanesia than the other Polynesian islands.

Its inhabitants believed in a western Havaiki from where their ancestors came; unlike the other Polynesians, however, they lacked a tradition of migration for the reason that in Polynesian terms Tonga and Samoa were the islands people sailed from rather than travelled to. Western Polynesia had no concept of a Sky Father and Earth Mother, nor did it have an organized pantheon of gods such as existed in New Zealand. As a result much of its mythology tended to revolve around lighter, more material concerns.

The Birth of Kava

Kava was a relaxing but non-intoxicating beverage that was consumed on ceremonial occasions. Kava drinking was particularly popular on Tonga, where it was said to have originated in a ludicrous comedy of manners. According to the story, a Tongan chief named Loua made a visit to a subsidiary chieftain on the island of Eueki. Unfortunately, Loua chose a bad moment: Eueki had just been hit by a gale that had destroyed its entire food supply save for one, bitter-tasting kape plant. Loua's host, Fevanga, was filled with embarrassment, but not wanting to lose face he decided to make what he could from the kape plant. Alas, Loua's men had carried his canoe up the beach and placed it right on top of the kape. Inveigling Loua into his small house, on the pretext that it would be cooler there, Fevanga hurriedly dug up the kape and made it into a near-palatable dish. Then a further problem presented itself. All the island's pigs and chickens had been killed and it would be exceptionally bad manners to offer Loua the kape without meat. Fevanga therefore took a club, killed his leprous daughter Kavaonau, and put her in the oven.

Loua thanked Fevanga for his kindness but was not fooled as to the meat. He told his host to give his daughter a proper burial, placing the head in one spot and the body in another. Five days later a kava plant sprouted from the head and a sugar cane grew from the body. Fevanga wondered what they could be for until he saw a rat chewing the plants. When it nibbled the kava it became light-headed and drowsy; when it ate the sugar cane, however, its vitality was restored. He reported this to Loua who laughed and gave instructions for the first kava ceremony to begin. He ordered people of low rank to split the kava and chew it to a pulp before straining the juice into a bowl through coconut husks. The bowl was then offered round with due protocol, starting with Loua and passing from him down the chain of seniority. Sugar cane was handed out, meanwhile, to counteract the kava's effect. As for future kava plants, they grew to grey and scaly maturity to remind people of their leprous origins.

The Duck and the Parrot-fish

Although the Western Polynesians had no tales of migration the sea still figured largely in their myths. One Tongan story told of the creation of the Magellan Clouds, the two bright patches by the Milky Way that sailors use as navigational aids. It started, in typically earthy fashion, with a chief named Maafu who was accustomed to make his morning toilet by a certain spring. Having wiped himself with a coconut husk he would throw the soiled article onto a nearby rock where it was devoured by a lizard. Eventually – if perplexingly – this diet made the lizard pregnant and she gave birth to two sons. As they grew the boys insisted

on meeting their father. They found him at a kava ceremony and introduced themselves as his sons. Maafu accepted them but never asked who their mother was for fear that – whoever she was – she should want to come and live with him as well.

The boys were sturdy but mischievous and, tiring of their rough behaviour, Maafu decided to dispense with their company. He instructed them to fetch water from a distant spring. What he did not tell them was that the spring was guarded by a terrifying duck that killed anyone who ventured near. The boys were equal to the challenge and returned not only with the water but with the duck too. Scowling, Maafu sent them to another spring inhabited by a ferocious, man-eating parrot-fish. They brought the fish back to him in triumph.

At that Maafu threw up his hands and told them they could have two separate pieces of land on the other side of Tonga if only they would

A view towards two islands of Tonga's Vava'u group at sunset, reminiscent of the separate land offered by Maafu to his sons. Instead, the boys opted to live in the arcing sky overhead.

promise to leave him alone. The boys came up with a better solution. If Maafu would give them the duck and the parrot-fish they would go and live in the sky in the Magellan Clouds, known on Tonga as Toloa and Humu, the duck and the parrot-fish. Maafu agreed and from that time on the father and his sons were able to see each other whenever they wanted without the awkwardness of actually meeting.

Sharks, Dolphins and One-upmanship

One tale that did involve migration ended not in the discovery of new land but the creation of a new god. It featured a boisterous Tongan youth

121

called Tu'i Tofua who was shouted at by his father for disturbing him as he was sleeping off a kava session. Deeply insulted, Tu'i Tofua vowed to go on a voyage and never return. Out on the waves he dared his crew to jump overboard. But the men knew that to do so would turn them into sharks; even so, keen to prove their manhood, they accepted his dare. Only one man held back. He was a Samoan, who rightly complained, "Who wants to grow up like a shark and be snared in a noose by fishermen and bashed with an oar, and cut up in pieces and shared out with the people while they clap their hands and scream and laugh.

Who wants that?" Tu'i Tofua saw his point and agreed that he need only cut off one of his fingers which would then become a porpoise. He sent the Samoan back to Tonga, then leaped into the sea and became a man-eating shark larger than all the rest. Thereafter he was worshipped as a god and it became a taboo to eat shark meat on Tonga.

In their telling, the tales of Maafu and Tu'i Tofua would have drawn winks and nudges from the audience, for they both dealt with a topic dear to the Tongan mind: the inferiority of Samoans. In the latter it was displayed by the Samoan's lack of pluck; in the former it was shown by the coconut

The Rat and the Bat

Unlike the rest of Polynesia, whose myths revolved mainly around the sea, Tonga and Samoa recounted tales of land mammals – among them the rat that cheated the fruit bat.

Although Tonga and Samoa had no greater variety of these creatures than other places save the relatively barren Chathams, their mythological presence maybe reflected a distant memory of life on the mainland.

One story that carried a rather depressing warning against being overtrustful towards friends told how the rat and the fruit bat changed roles. The rat was envious of the fruit bat's wings and devised a stratagem whereby it could acquire them. Watching the fruit bat to see which berries it liked best, the rat positioned itself under an ifi tree, and when the bat came

to eat the rat asked it why it was trespassing on its personal food supply. Sweeping aside the bat's apologies, the rat said it did not mind too much and that they should both be friends. As a sign of their friendship the rat would let the bat eat from the ifi tree; all it asked in return was to borrow the bat's wings so that it could experience flight.

The bat reluctantly consented to the request and handed over its wings with the warning that the rat must not be too long. The rat gave the bat its paws and tail to look after, then soared into the sky never to be seen again. Thereafter, whenever one Samoan chief cheated another, the people would say, "But did you not know of the friendship of the bat and the rat?"

Various naturalistic forms of marine life – what appear to be sharks, whales and dolphins – are incorporated in the design of this Tongan barkcloth, or *tapa*. An ancient craft, *tapa*-making was normally the work of women, although men prepared it for use on ritual objects such as masks and loincloths.

husk being tossed onto a rock – whereas Tongan males used husk and females *tapa* cloth, it was well-known that the "lowly" Samoans used stones. The rivalry between the two islands was so deeply rooted that one Tongan myth gave it divine origins. In a distant time, Tonga had coconuts but no chickens, whereas Samoa had chickens but no coconuts. Their gods agreed to do a swap. The Samoan god, however, tried to trick his counterpart by dressing up an owl as a chicken. Expecting something of the sort, the Tongan god sliced open a coconut and scooped out its flesh to leave only an empty shell. The exchange having been concluded, the Samoan god chortled, "Farewell, with owl-fowl." At that the Tongan god delivered his barbed, sexual riposte: "Farewell, with cut-nut." Needless to say, the same tale was told in Samoa but with the characters and outcome reversed.

Despite their one-upmanship, Tongans and Samoans had more in common than they liked to admit. Just as Tu'i Tofua was considered the ancestor of sharks on Tonga, so a Samoan chief named Li'ava'a was believed to be the creator of dolphins. It was his custom to drink kava at sea, so when one day he wanted to go fishing Li'ava'a told his daughter Sina to prepare the drink. He was well into the trip when he asked Sina to bring out the kava. When there was no response he called again. At this juncture his men pointed out that he had left Sina behind. Magisterially, Li'ava'a commanded them to swim back to shore and fetch the kava. On entering the water they became dolphins but no sooner did they reach the beach where Sina stood, beckoning them in with a white fan, than they were hauled ashore by the islanders and eaten. In Samoa, stranded dolphins were explained by this endless but doomed quest to fulfil their chief's command. Their arrival was traditionally celebrated by a young girl standing on the beach with a white fan in imitation of Sina.

123

The Closeness of the Sea

Outlying islands and atolls were the last parts of Polynesia to be affected by Western influence. Some were not disturbed until the twentieth century, making their myths the area's purest and least adulterated. At their heart lay a simplicity that underpinned atoll life.

A precarious ring of land surrounding an inner lagoon, an atoll was rarely more than three metres above sea level or more than a few hundred metres across. Topographically and in every other way, it was devoid of extremes. The main food-sources were plentiful but unexciting: coconuts, breadfruit, fish, seabirds' eggs and occasionally the odd turtle. Society was equally basic: the land could sustain only a limited number of people; there was no wealth to be accumulated; and as a consequence there was little power to be wielded. Existence was a matter of cooperation; haughtiness and greed were despised. This even, tranquil world was prevented from slipping into monotony only by the tempestuous gales that sometimes swept the Pacific. The natural diffidence of atoll dwellers was exemplified in a series of myths recorded on Kapingamarangi in 1947; every one of them ended with the words, "*Waranga tangata hua*" – "Just a tale that people tell."

Atoll dwellers were closer – literally – to the sea than any other people on Earth and sea creatures featured prominently in their mythology. One tale told how the lobster and the flounder earned their distinguishing features in a game of hide-and-seek. The flounder was able to spot the lobster easily because of its protruding feelers. When it was the lobster's turn to seek, however, the flounder buried itself invisibly in the sand. The lobster was so angry at being outwitted that it jumped up and down on the flounder's head, driving one of its eyes into the grit. The flounder complained that it could not see, so the lobster gouged out the eye and stuck it haphazardly on top of its head. Ironically, humans can always spot lobsters because of their feelers but the flounder is able to hide because of its two upward-facing eyes.

If atoll dwellers were different from other Polynesians they still shared a number of legends with their island cousins, among them the memory of life arriving from across the ocean. According to one story, Tikopia atoll was initially inhabited only

This volcanic island is ringed by coral to form a lagoon. While the reef is typical, atolls usually lie much lower in the water.

by women who bred with bats to produce yet more women. Then a man arrived from over the seas. His name was "Swift Whistling". He killed and ate the bats, mated with the women and produced a race of humans that included males.

Taboos were also known on the atolls. A tale from Kapingamarangi recounted an episode in which a woman named Riuta went fishing with her husband, Tuikoro, and ignored his injunction to wash her hands only on the outrigger side of the canoe. When she broke the taboo a spirit woman arose from the sea and took her place beside her. Tuikoro turned round, saw two women looking exactly alike and threw Riuta overboard thinking she was the spirit. Riuta, who was pregnant, swam to a nearby atoll and gave birth to twin boys. They grew up and made their way to where their father was living with Riuta's double. On hearing their chant Tuikoro knew that he had made a mistake and with his sons' help burned the spirit woman's house to the ground before sailing with them to the atoll. As a surprise for their mother, Tuikoro told the boys to wrap him in a sail and carry him ashore as if they had been on an innocent fishing voyage. When he was set down on the beach he would spring out and fill his wife with delight.

Elsewhere in Polynesia the saga might have ended happily, but on Kapingamarangi it carried a moral. Riuta realized Tuikoro was hiding in the sail and in return for his ill-treatment of her she dashed it onto the rocks, killing him. In the story's final words, "That is all. Just a tale people tell."

Maui the Trickster Hero

One of the most popular figures in Polynesian mythology was the trickster hero Maui. Rebel, seducer and social iconoclast, Maui flaunted conventions, toppled hierarchies and broke taboos. He was seen as the defender of the weak and the protector of the underprivileged. Such was his fame that one of the Hawaiian islands was named after him.

Even in birth, Maui was different from others. Born prematurely, the result of a miscarriage, he was wrapped in a lock of his mother's hair and thrown into the sea. Many Polynesians believed that embryos became mischievous spirits and Maui was no exception. Rescued by the sun god, this half-human demigod was reunited with his mother and almost immediately began to turn life on its head.

Giver and Creator

One of Maui's first feats was to slow down the passage of the sun by beating it with the jawbone of his dead grandmother so that it was forced to crawl across the sky, thus giving his mother more time in which to beat *tapa* cloth. Some say he achieved this feat by catching the sun in a snare made from the hair of his sister, Hina-ika. Other versions told how he delayed the sun's progress so that humans might have more time for cooking.

Maui provided humans with resources and skills. His name comes from the word for the left, profane side of the body, rather than the sacred, right or *tapa* side. This is reflected in his unconventional behaviour. This oblique profile carving, made for the Rauru meeting house, shows Maui's most spectacular exploit, fishing up the land.

126

As the hero of the common man it was only natural that Maui should be associated with such everyday tasks as cooking and cloth-making. In the same vein, he was credited with bringing fire to the world. Descending to the underworld, he tricked the goddess Mahui-ike into discarding her burning fingernails, from which fire came. When she had only one fingernail left, she flung it to the ground in anger. Maui called for rain to extinguish the blaze, but the goddess preserved the sacred spark by throwing it onto a nearby stand of trees. She thereby taught Maui a great secret which he bore triumphantly back to humankind: wood could be used to make fire.

Other tales link Maui to features in the landscape – even the creation of land itself. In Tonga there is a great stone trilithon monument more than five metres in height said to have been brought to the island by Maui. In New Zealand it was related that he made the islands surface on a fishing trip. Out on the ocean with his brothers, Maui fell asleep leaving his bait dangling in the water. When he awoke, he hauled up the line

Sentient Creatures

Alongside the gods and their semi-divine or human offspring Polynesia embraced a body of intermediate spiritual beings. Not quite "fairies" in the European sense, they were usually fair-skinned creatures who lurked in forests or on hills and who interfered for good or evil in human affairs. They were also portrayed as malevolent ogres, enchanted goblins or evil fish.

The *patupaiarehe*, as Maoris called theses sentient people, had fair, tattoo-free skin. It is possible they had their origin in tales of the indigenous populace displaced by Polynesian immigration who took refuge in less habitable zones. Either way, the *patupaiarehe* were considered non-human and were shunned as a treacherous and crafty influence – though their plaintive flutes exercised a magnetic effect on women and could result in disruptive inter-marriages.

In parts of Polynesia their fair skin was thought to resemble the pallor of death and they were seen as the lingering spirits of those who had been unable or unwilling to find a final resting place. These spirits could be encountered anywhere – usually at night – but were most often found in remote parts of the forest where they would surprise root-gatherers with a menacing whisper: "You rejoice today, but my turn will come tomorrow."

Spirits were normally viewed as being small to medium sized. Sometimes, though, they assumed the form of mighty humans who could stride from island to island, or of gigantic birds and fish who menaced men and women as they went about their everyday activities.

and found he had caught something so monstrous that it was more the size of an island than a fish. He and his brothers grappled with it but it broke free and fell back into the sea. Maui threw out his hook again – on some islands the hook was said to be the same jawbone with which he had cudgelled the sun – but once more he was unable to control the mighty fish. On his third try he was successful and he set its body in the water where it became New Zealand's North Island. Maui's canoe became the top of the island's highest mountain, Hikurangi, and his hook was immortalized as a crescent-shaped bay called Hawke Bay. As for the fish, its skin began to wither and crinkle in the sun, giving rise to the hilly folds that characterize North Island.

Forever Mortal

Maui was a mythological huckster – his title, Maui of 1,000 Tricks, carried more than a whiff of showmanship – and as such, not everything he did turned out well. Once, he managed to turn his brother-in-law into the first dog. Another time, he tried to achieve immortality by having sex with the goddess of death. The result was disastrous.

It was said that a man approaching death was "creeping into the womb of Sleeping Mother Death", meaning returning to the dark womb of the earth. While wandering through the underworld with his friends, Maui chanced upon the sleeping figure of Hine-nui-te-Po, the giant goddess of death. Maui was delighted, for his mother had told him that should he crawl through Hine's womb and emerge through her mouth then the goddess would die and death would no longer exist. Cautioning silence, Maui stripped off and climbed bodily inside Hine. But halfway through the act he became stuck, a sight that caused his friends much hilarity. In fact, one of them – a bird – laughed so loudly that the goddess woke up. Hine squeezed Maui to death inside her and in return for his impudence she confirmed that humankind would forever remain mortal. From that time every man and woman was doomed to end his or her life in Hine's clutches.

127

The Afterworld

Humans may have lost their chance of immortality thanks to Maui's ill-judged actions (see page 127), but if their bodies died, their souls lived on obstinately. It was widely agreed that the soul went to an afterworld, but ideas about what form it took varied.

Death played an important, if grudgingly acknowledged, role in Polynesian society. Corpses were prayed for, sung to, wept over – in New Zealand tears were said to "avenge death" – and provided with a panoply of sacrifices and ritual chants to ensure their souls reached the afterworld successfully. They might then be buried, or left to disintegrate until nothing but the skeleton remained, whereupon the bones would be stored in carved boxes and placed in a sacred site. On atolls, which had a lack of sites either secular or sacred, the bones were hung from the meeting house rafters.

The corpse having been disposed of, there remained only the question of where the soul went. In general the afterworld was considered synonymous with the underworld, the Havaiki from which Polynesians had first arrived. It was there that the soul travelled, following a path marked by recognizable geographical features. In New Zealand, for example, the *wairua* or soul made its way to the northernmost tip of the mainland, crossing en route streams and beaches with names such as Waters of Lamentation and Twilight Sands. At the final promontory it climbed down to the ocean and swam out to the island of Ohau, visible in the distance. Here it ascended the highest hill for a final glimpse of the land it would never see again, then made its way westwards towards the setting sun and the land of its ancestors.

The afterworld was not necessarily a single unit but could comprise several layers, each governed by its own divinity. (Some islanders even believed in separate afterworlds for animals – Tahiti had one for pigs.) The layers were divided into "heavens" and "hells" – the Marquesans had four of the latter, the Maoris ten – but these categories had none of the moral associations of Western culture. They simply reflected the dead person's status when alive and the quality of sacrifices made by his or her descendants. There was

In Polynesia it was believed that the spirits of the dead walked away along a path across the sea towards the setting sun. In New Zealand dead people's souls headed towards a headland above the northern beaches to gather and travel together across the ocean to Havaiki.

little sense of judgement involved. Death was the continuation of life in another world and the difference in social conditions for the dead was just the same as for the living.

Once in the afterworld the soul became an object of worship. All Polynesians looked to the spirits of their ancestors to protect and advise them, and often sought their aid in preference to that of the gods themselves. There were some souls, however, who never reached their destination – usually through neglected funeral rites – or who returned because they envied the living. These malign demons trailed calamity in their wake and reminded people that however little the afterworld may have differed from the real one, death was still a terrible and frightening thing. In New Zealand the house in which a person died had to be burned down, although this taboo was approached with a certain pragmatism: if someone fell ill in an expensive, ceremonial dwelling, he or she was quickly shifted to a cheap shack.

The question of where the soul went after death would have been irrelevant had it not been for the creation of death itself. Many myths stated that humankind had once been immortal and was plunged into its present state only by divine – or, in Maui's case, semi-divine – shenanigans. Often sexual, and always involving females, the tales usually linked death with the moment of birth and one of the oldest of them concerned Hine-titama.

Hine-titama's Haven

In one of the oldest stories, death came about as a result of the half-human goddess Hine-titama giving birth to a child by her father, the creator-god Tane (see page 105).

At first Hine did not realize that her supposed husband was in fact her father. But in time she became suspicious and Tane's evasive replies to her questions told her all she needed to know. She thereupon departed for the underworld to create a place where her descendants would be forever safe from Tane's ravages. She chanted spells to weaken Tane's power and send their children to sleep – a state that was widely considered to represent temporary death. Before she left, however, she planted an Adam's apple in Tane's throat both as a farewell gift and as a mark of the difference that would thereafter exist between the two mortal sexes. Her last words to him were, "Remain, O Tane, to pull our offspring to day, while I go to drag them down to night."

Parlaying her way through the guardians of the underworld, she succeeded in creating a haven where her children's souls could outlive their mortal shells. "Let me remain", she begged the final guardian, "that I may catch the living spirits of my descendants in the world of everlasting light." He consented and Hine built a comfortable refuge in the World Below for those who had fled the World of Light.

The Mysteries of Easter Island

Isolated in the easternmost corner of Polynesia, Easter Island was known to its inhabitants as "The Navel of the World". Measuring only 117 square kilometres and separated from its nearest neighbour – tiny Pitcairn Island – by 2,400 kilometres of ocean, it nevertheless had some right to this title for it differed so radically from the rest of Polynesia.

To this day, scholars puzzle over two aspects of Easter Island: the massive stone statues that once dotted its slopes; and the existence, unique in Polynesia, of a written script (see page 117). Unfortunately, the arrival of slavers and diseases after the European discovery decimated the population to such an extent that by 1914 there was only one man left who could explain the statues or the scripts. He died without divulging his secrets, thereby plunging Easter Island into mystery.

In orally transmitted lore the Easter Islanders ascribed their genesis to a bird's egg from which humankind hatched. Naturally, therefore, birds played an important part in their life and were placed under the protection of the god Makemake, half-bird and half-man. Every year a "bird man" was appointed who enjoyed high ceremonial prestige and was awarded a potent fertility charm comprising an egg stuffed with *tapa* cloth.

In common with other Polynesians the Easter Islanders told of their initial arrival from a distant homeland to the west – known not as Havaiki but as Marae Renga, a name which carried connotations of worship. The driving force was a chief named Hotu Matua whose tattooer had dreamed of a land that had two prominent features: a large hole (a volcanic crater) and beaches of white sand. Hotu Matua sent six boats to find this promising place and in due course they landed on an island that had not only a crater but the sand of which the tattooer had spoken. Hotu Matua followed in their wake, bringing all the essentials for life. From his canoe came birds, turtles, yams, gourds, crayfish, bananas and the aute tree from which *tapa* was made – not to mention hundreds of humans.

Like New Zealand, Easter Island also had a myth to explain its heritage of carving. The originator was a priest-cum-navigator named Tu'u Ko Ihu who one day chanced upon two male spirits asleep. They looked like dead men, so gaunt and fleshless that their ribs showed. Stealing away without waking them, Tu'u Ko Ihu carved their likeness in wood. That night he dreamed of women who covered their genitals with their

The title of "bird man" was given to the man who found the first sea bird's egg of the season. These bird-man petroglyphs are on the sacred boulders at Orongo on the rim of Rano Kau crater.

A large ritual effigy figure, more than 40cm tall, whose exact purpose remains a mystery, although it was probably associated with burial and represented an ancestor. The wrapping made it *tapu* (or taboo) while its lineage invested it with *mana*.

hands. The next morning he carved them in wood in the same posture. From that time all Easter Island carvings were similar: the men were portrayed with a rack of prominent ribs while the women were shown in a position of modesty.

The wooden carvings of Easter Island bore little resemblance, however, to the massive stone heads and torsos that were strewn over the mountainside. The centrepieces of temple sites known as *ahu*, these lantern-jawed effigies, topped with sacred red limestone, held one clue as to their origins – their ears were often pendulous, as if elongated by the insertion of heavy objects.

Mainland South American nobles from Peru were "long-eared" whereas the Polynesians were not. The possibility of Peruvians having made the long journey, subduing the population and erecting statues in their own image. is reinforced by a myth that tells of a battle between the native "short-ears" and a temple-building caste of rulers called the "long-ears".

According to tradition the "long-ears" controlled all the best land, relegating the "short-ears" to the most barren and stony ground. The arrangement was to the "long-ears'" economic advantage. It was also to their spiritual benefit, for the stones that the "short-ears" dug from their fields could be used for temple construction. The "short-ears" cleared their fields but refused to haul the stones to the designated temple sites – that task they left to their overlords. Resentfully, the "long-ears" built the temples themselves. Then they started on a new project that took the form of a long trench filled with firewood. The "short-ears" were baffled as to its purpose until one woman who had married a "long-ear" learned from her husband that the ditch was nothing but a mass grave into which all "short-ears" were to be thrown before being cooked and eaten. Forewarned, the "short-ears" rose against their masters. They lit the firewood, then drove the "long-ears" into the trench. Only two "long-ears" survived the flames. One was allowed to join the community. The other, jabbering an incomprehensible language, was thrown into the leper colony to breed as he wished.

THE BEAUTY OF TATTOOING

Permanent decoration of the body and face was ritually practised on both sexes throughout Oceania, but particularly in Melanesia and Polynesia where tattooing was an expression of concern with the body, social status and *mana*. To the Maori (who called it *ta moko*) and others, the art was a divine gift (see pages 112–113), and was usually the preserve of a specific class. Most designs were created using bones which held ink (soot and oil) on a serrated edge and were tapped with hammers to puncture the skin. An alternative method, unique to the Maori, involved curvilinear chiselling of the skin to inscribe the tattoo in a similar manner to their elaborate decoration of wood.

Above: Many modern Maori people, such as Vicki Te Amo, are helping to revive traditional tattooing practices in New Zealand.

Right: An unidentified Maori chief, his face incised with traditional swirling designs. The cloak he wears is of a type said to have originally been a gift to the Maori from Uetonga, who also revealed to Mataroa the art of tattooing. In many parts of Oceania, only elite men had the right to a full-facial tattoo.

Below: This Marshall Islands square mat, woven from leaves, dates from the 1920s. The geometric border designs represent traditional, divinely ordained tattoo patterns which distinguish family identity, rank and social status.

Right: This intricately carved Maori *korere* or feeding funnel was used to give broth and water to a person undergoing facial tattoo. No solids were allowed in case the skin became contaminated.

Far right: This panel by Tene Waitere, *c.*1899, shows examples of facial tattoos for both sexes. Maori women rarely had the status for a full-face *moko*, receiving instead *moko* on the lip, chin and between the eyebrows, perhaps with incising on the nostrils.

THE OCEANIAN LEGACY

Over the past two centuries the South Pacific world has been transformed by the arrival of Europeans. The first explorers arrived much earlier than that – as far back as 1521 in the case of Ferdinand de Magellan's landfall on Guam in the Marianas. But for the next 250 years, contact was rare. It was only in the second half of the eighteenth century, following the well-publicized voyages of the French navigator Louis de Bougainville and, even more, of England's Captain James Cook, that Western interest was truly aroused.

In three voyages between 1768 and 1779, Cook charted New Zealand and the east coast of Australia and explored Antarctica. Like Bougainville before him, he also visited Tahiti, and the enthusiastic reports the two brought back about its climate, landscape and people – Bougainville called it the New Cythera, after the famed classical island of love – did as much as anything else to stimulate European interest in the southern ocean.

Another decisive step occurred in 1788, when the British decided to establish a penal colony in Australia. This permanent white presence ensured that nothing would ever be quite the same again.

Transformation

In a few short years, the newcomers radically transformed the societies they found. Tahiti – so enticingly advertised by the early voyagers – felt the brunt sooner than most. Venereal disease arrived on the island with the first ships, and other ailments rapidly followed. So too did rifles, which turned tribal conflicts, traditionally fought with clubs and spears, into altogether more lethal affairs. Within thirty years of Cook's landfall, the population had been reduced from around 40,000 to 16,000. Over the next half-century it was to fall further, eventually stabilizing at about 6,000.

Paul Gauguin's *Man with Axe* shows male and female Tahitians at work, c.1891. The French painter spent a decade in Tahiti and his artistic output was heavily influenced by the rich colours and stylized artistic tradition of the island.

Traditional customs were drastically altered too. Missionaries arrived in the wake of the explorers, and the confused and demoralized islanders were in no shape to resist their message. The dramatic change they brought about was chronicled by a Russian navigator who visited Tahiti in 1820. He reported that no one danced or played music any more; even the weaving of flower garlands was forbidden. The old myths and beliefs had been largely swept away. Both men and women shaved their heads, and the traditional art of tattooing had been discouraged. Sex outside marriage was a crime, and moral guardians wandered the countryside on the lookout for illicit lovers.

Settlers followed close behind the missionaries. Some were idealists who imagined the islands as lands of primeval innocence unsullied by civilization's deadening hand. Their numbers included the writers Herman Melville and Robert Louis Stevenson and the painter Paul Gauguin, all of whom were more or less disillusioned with the sadly altered societies they actually found. Many more came in search of easy profits, and exploitation was soon added to the islanders' other woes.

The conclusion of the process came in the latter part of the nineteenth and early twentieth centuries, when colonial administrators moved in. Colonies or protectorates were established by the British, French, Dutch, German and American governments. The southern seas had effectively been annexed, and the old Oceania was no more.

In Australia, the European intrusion was both more abrupt and more lethal for the indigenous peoples. The penal colony established in 1788 proved the prologue to British occupation of the entire continent. To justify expropriation, the incomers had recourse to the legal doctrine of *terra nullius*, which proclaimed that the land had no previous owners. Conflict inevitably ensued, and the Aborigines, with their limited armoury of spears and clubs, were necessarily the losers.

For some local populations the results of the clash of cultures were terminal. The most extreme case was Tasmania, where near-genocide took place (see page 10); but similar encounters on a

Many cultural traditions were never lost, while others have been revived by resurgent indigenous cultures throughout the Pacific. Here, Queen Elizabeth II is provided with a Tuvalu welcome.

less apocalyptic scale occurred elsewhere across the Australian landmass. When white control was firmly established over the continent, the surviving Aborigines were persecuted, forbidden to own land, had no vote in elections and were not counted in censuses, while their children rarely received any schooling. A common assumption was that they would follow the example of the Tasmanians and simply fade away.

Indigenous Renaissance

In fact things turned out very differently. The years after World War II saw a revival in numbers and morale. In part the change was due to improved access to health care and a decrease in infant mortality. By 1971, when Aborigines were first included in the census, there were reckoned to be 140,000 in the country. Present assessments suggest that numbers are approaching 300,000 – the estimated population at the time that white settlers first arrived two centuries ago.

Pacific Islanders have unerringly managed to adopt and adapt outside influences – witness this shield in which the artist, Kaipel, has subtly altered a lager advert to refer to clan rivalries.

Increased self-confidence has been reflected in a growing political awareness. Aborigines only got the vote in 1962, but soon an active campaign for land rights was under way. Legislation granting limited tenure followed in 1977, although the issue remains very much alive today.

At the same time, something of a cultural revolution has taken place as a fresh generation of white Australians has made common cause with the Aborigines in an attempt to come to terms with the continent in which they find themselves living. The new sensibility expressed itself in such films of the 1970s as *Picnic at Hanging Rock* and *The Last Wave* which subtly hinted at age-old mysteries underlying the surface of Australian life that only the Aborigines could comprehend. Similar sentiments informed *The Songlines*, a 1987 travelogue by the English author Bruce Chatwin.

Such works stimulated new interest in the Aborigines' own culture, which has experienced something of a renaissance in recent years. Paintings by Aborigine artists sell well on the international art market, and the Australian airline Qantas has chosen Pitjantjarra designs to decorate its aircraft's fuselages. There are Aborigine pop groups and dance troupes, and there has even been a brief cult of the didjeridoo in World Music circles. All these manifestations reflect a newly positive mood that is transforming the people's badly damaged self-image. For the first time since the European irruption, Australia's first inhabitants can feel that they have a future as well as a past.

In New Zealand the process of recovery had begun rather earlier. Maori rights were at least nominally respected following the signing of the Treaty of Waitangi between representatives of the British government and local chiefs in 1840. Even so, the effects of contact in terms of declining populations and the alienation of tribal lands was not that different from the Australian experience. The population reached a low of about 45,000 at the end of the nineteenth century, by which time white settlers owned 85 per cent of the land.

The revival was spearheaded politically early in the twentieth century by the Young Maori Party. Since then the indigenous people have increasingly made their presence felt at the heart of national life. One very visible sign of their presence is the *haka* war dance performed before each match by the All Blacks rugby team, New Zealand's foremost sporting ambassadors. Even so, integration has left a legacy of social problems, as memorably revealed in the award-winning 1995 film *Once Were Warriors*.

The situation in Oceania today varies from island to island, current political status being partially shaped by the action of the Western colonial powers. As a result, political divisions are often arbitrary. So the western half of New Guinea, once Dutch territory, is now Irian Jaya, a constituent part of Indonesia, while the eastern section is the independent state of Papua New Guinea.

This huge island, home to almost two-thirds of Oceania's total population, was in fact historically something of a special case, as its difficult terrain combined with the fierce reputation of its inhabitants to discourage European settlement. It was only in the 1930s, when light aircraft opened up the interior, that white influence made itself felt.

The most dramatic responses were the cargo cults that spread across New Guinea and neighbouring islands in the years before World War II. The consumer goods the white men brought with them seemed like treasure trove to the indigenous peoples who, seeing them descend from the heavens in aeroplanes, not illogically came to the conclusion that they were gifts from sky spirits.

Following the rationale of this belief, some groups cleared mock landing strips on their territories and mimicked the clothes and bearing of Westerners in the hope that the bounty would start to come their way. Others made shrines of the crates in which the goods arrived. Some of the cults took on a millenarian aspect, leading villagers to tear up the gardens on which their sustenance depended in the belief that a golden age of plenty was about to dawn. When it failed to materialize,

hope turned to anger, leaving many convinced that the Europeans were appropriating assets intended for local people. The cults faded away in the 1940s as the exoticism of the newcomers diminished.

Excluding Hawaii and New Guinea, Oceania has only around 2.5 million inhabitants. In general acculturation has been most marked in the islands of Micronesia, where American military influence has been strong. In Polynesia some groups, such as the kingdom of Tonga which has been ruled by one dynasty since 1845, have kept closer to their roots, though even there traditional ways have largely succumbed to modern-world pressures.

More than a century ago, Stevenson and Melville discovered the traditional South Seas' cultures in disarray. Today they would find them changed beyond recognition. Yet if some of the old ways of life have gone for ever, memories of the crafts associated with them, together with the myths that helped give them meaning, have not died; in fact, government-backed forums like the quadrennial Festival of Pacific Arts are encouraging something of a revival. Very few people in the South Pacific region still explain their lives in terms of the old stories; but there is still an impulse to treasure them and see that they are not forgotten.

The Aboriginal band Yothu Yindi have fused traditional music with rock to create a popular World Music sound.

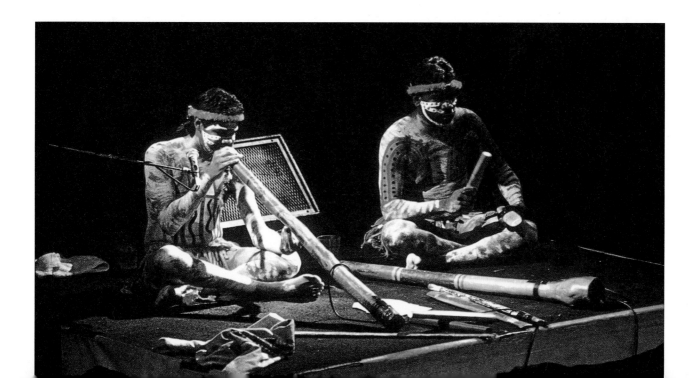

Glossary

Altjeringa The Dreamtime; an age at the dawn of the world when the land was moulded and filled with its various animal and plant life.

ahu Easter Island burial and ceremonial platforms or temple sites.

Aotearoa The Maori word for New Zealand, or traditionally its North Island, generally translated as "Land of the Long White Cloud".

bilum A feather bag version, made partly by mothers in New Guinea for their sons initiation, of the sacred bone container created by the spirit heroine Afek.

birrimbirr Two separate souls were believed by some Aborigines to leave the human body after death, and this soul was the one that lingered among the living.

djang Magical ancestral energy or primal power stored in a specific place or feature of the sacred landscape.

haka A Maori posture dance.

hei-tiki or tiki See *tiki*.

korere A Maori feeding funnel used when an individual underwent facial tattooing. A similar word – *korero* – meant "conversation" or "story".

mana A word that was used throughout the region to signify a spiritual force which could be vested in both people and objects, to give power, prestige or authority.

marae Polynesian ceremonial ground, usually situated at the centre of a village. Among the Maori it was located in front of the tribal meeting house.

moai maea Massive stone sculptures which stood atop Easter Island's *ahu* platforms and formed their centrepiece.

moiety A group of clans within an Aboriginal tribal community.

moko, ta moko Maori tattooing.

mokuy Of the two separate souls believed by some Aborigines to leave the body after death, this one journeyed to an afterworld.

pa A fortified Maori stronghold.

pare In Maori culture, a decoratively carved panel or lintel.

patupaiarehe Fair-skinned spirit creatures who, in Maori lore, lived in remote areas and could interfere malevolently in human affairs.

poutokamanawa Maori central interior housepost that supported the ridgepole and combined the figure of a tribal ancestor.

rangga The sacred, ancestral tribal objects that belonged to Arnhem Land's Yolngu Aboriginal people.

rongorongo Easter Island sacred script of engraved glyphs recorded on cloth or bark.

tahu'a Priestly teachers of the Society Islands who taught a wide range of subjects, reflected in their name which meant "Cave of many outlets".

tapa A form of Pacific Island barkcloth, often used for ritual objects.

tapu Something sacred which was restricted or prohibited and therefore unavailable or inaccessible to many on pain of punishment (the word "taboo" is derived from it). Also in places it meant the quality of being invested with *mana*.

terra nullius Legal doctrine that proclaimed the land of Australia had no previous owners.

tiki or hei-tiki A *tiki* was a Maori carved human figure; a *hei-tiki* was a pendant of a stylized ancestor figure associated with fertility and usually made of green stone. In the Society Islands they were called *ti'i*.

wairua A Maori word for "spirit" or "soul".

waka Maori sea-going canoes, associated with their original migration and also used to mean a loose association of tribes.

wharenui Maori meeting house.

yipwon A New Guinea spirit figure that assisted men in hunting.

Index

Page numbers in *italic* denote captions. Where there is a textual reference to the topic on the same page as a caption, italics have not been used.

143

Further Reading

Alpers, Antony. *The World of the Polynesians*, Oxford University Press: Auckland, 1987

Berndt, R.M. and Berndt, C.H. *The First Australians*, Sydney University Press: Sydney, 1952

Berndt, R.M. and Berndt, C.H. *Aboriginal Australian Art*, New Holland Publishers Ltd: Frenchs Forest, New South Wales, 1998

Craig, R.D. *Dictionary of Polynesian Mythology*, Greenwood Press: New York, 1989

D'Alleva. *Art of the Pacific*, The Everyman Art Library: London, 1998

Hiatt, L.R. (ed.) *Australian Aboriginal Mythology*, Australian Institute of Aboriginal Studies: Canberra, 1975

Kame'eleiwiha, L. *Native Land and Foreign Desires*, Bishop Museum Press, 1992

Kirch, P. *Feathered Gods and Fishhooks*, University of Hawaii Press, 1985

Knappert, Jan. *Pacific Mythology*, Diamond Books: London, 1995

Morphy, H. *Ancestral Connections*, Chicago University Press: Chicago, 1991

Mudrooroo. *Aboriginal Mythology*, Thorsons: London, 1994

Mulvaney, D.J. and White, J.P. (eds.) *Australians to 1788*, Fairfax, Syme & Weldon Associates: Broadway, New South Wales, 1987

Nile, Richard and Clerk, Christian. *Cultural Atlas of Australia, New Zealand and the South Pacific*, Facts on File: New York, 1996

Orbell, Margaret. *The Illustrated Encyclopedia of Maori Myths and Legend*, Canterbury University Press: Christchurch, 1995

Robinson, Roland. *Legend & dreaming*, Edwards & Shaw: Sydney, 1952

Starzecka, D.C. (ed.) *Maori Art and Culture*, British Museum Press: London, 1996

Thomas, Nicholas. *Oceanic Art*, Thames and Hudson: London, 1995

Yikmikirli. (trans. P.R. Napaljarri and L. Cataldi) *Warlpiri Dreamings and Histories*, Harper Collins: San Francisco, 1994

Picture Credits

t = top, c = centre, b = bottom, l = left, r = right

Bridgeman Art Library, London/New York = BAL
British Museum, London = BM
Berndt Museum of Anthology, Australia = BMA
Christie's Images, London = Christie's
Images Colour Library, London = Images

Natural History Photographic Agency, England = NHPL
Royal Geographical Society, London = RGS
Robert Harding Picture Library, London = RHPL
Werner Forman Archive, London = WFA

Cover National Museum of New Zealand, Wellington/WFA; **Cover border** Christine Osborne Pictures; **title page** Colorific, London; **contents page** Christie's; **page 6** Penny Tweedie /Colorific; **7** Christie's; **8–9** J.C Callow/Panos Pictures, London; **10–11** BMA; **11** National Library of Australia, Canberra/BAL; **15** Christie's; **16** Pitt Rivers Museum, University of Oxford; **16–17** BM; **18** Phillip Goldman Collection, London/WFA; **19tr** WFA/Auckland Institute and Museum; **19br** Tim Graham Picture Library, London; **19bl** John Miles/RGS; **20** Images; **21** Institut fur Ethnologie der Universitat Gottingen, Germany; **22** Peter Barker/Colorific; **23** Images; **24** BMA; **25** RHPL; **26** John Miles/RGS **27** Popperfoto, London; **28** Larsen Collinge Int/RHPL; **30** Louise Murray/RHPL; **33** BMA; **34** BMA; **35** National Gallery of Australia, Canberra; **36–37** BMA; **38** Wade Hughes/Lochmann Transparencies, Western Australia; **39** Penny Tweedie/Panos Pictures; **42** Max Alexander, London; **44** Col Roberts/Lochmann Transparencies; **45** Takarakka Rock Art Centre, Australia; **46** Penny Tweedie/Panos Pictures; **48–49** J.C Callow/Panos Pictures; **49t** Bill Bachmann, Victoria, Australia; **49br** John Miles/RGS; **50l** Denis Sarson/Lochmann Transparencies; **50–51** Christine Osborne Pictures, London; **51tr** Andre Singer/The Hutchison Library, London; **51b** Penny Tweedie/Panos Pictures; **52** Penny Tweedie/Panos Pictures; **53** BMA; **55** National Gallery of Australia, Canberra; **56** Peter Barker/Panos Pictures ; **57** BMA; **58–59** Penny Tweedie/Network, London; **62** Graham Walsh/Takarakka Rock Art Centre; **63** BMA; **64** Coo-ee Picture Library, Victoria, Australia; **65tl** Denis Sarson/Lochmann Transparencies; **65tr** Jiri Lochmann/Lochmann Transparencies; **67** Art Gallery of New South Wales, Sydney; **68** Robert Francis/RHPL; **69** Christie's; **70** Otto Rogers/NHPL; **72** Robert Francis/The Hutchison Library; **74** John Shaw/NHPL; **75** Coo-ee Picture Library; **76** RGS; **77** Pitt Rivers Museum; **78** Tony Stone Images; **78–79** Christopher Arnesen/Tony Stone Images; **79tl** RHPL; **79r** Oliver Strewe/Tony Stone Images; **80** Paul Harris/RGS; **81** Christie's; **82–83** Museum Volkerkunde, Basel/Colorphoto Hinz, Germany; **84** Colorphoto Hinz; **86** Christie's; **87** Christie's; **88** Phillip Goldman Collection, London/WFA; **89** S.Sassoon/RHPL; **90** Otago Museum, Dunedin, New Zealand; **91** Christie's; **92** Norbert Wu/NHPL; **93** Courtesy Entwistle Gallery, London/WFA; **94** Courtesy Entwistle Gallery/WFA; **96tl** National Maritime Museum, London/BAL; **96bl** National Museum of New Zealand, Wellington; **96r** Phillip Goldman Collection/WFA; **97** Glen Allison/Tony Stone Images; **98** National Museum of New Zealand/WFA; **99** Bruce Coleman Limited, England; **100** Collection of the Museum of New Zealand Te Papa Tongarewa, B.18915, Wellington; **101** BM; **102** Pitt Rivers Museum; **104** BM; **105** Bruce Coleman Limited; **106–107** Images; **108** BM; **109** Courtesy Entwistle Gallery, London/WFA; **110** Otago Museum, /WFA; **112** BM/WFA; **113** Museum fur Volderkunde, Berlin/WFA; **114** BM; **115** National Maritime Museum/e.t.archive, London; **116** Bruce Coleman Collection; **117** Pitt Rivers Museum; **121** James Strachan/RHPL; **123** Auckland Museum, New Zealand; **124–125** Jean-Marc Truchet/Tony Stone Images; **126** Hamburg Museum fur Volkerkunde; **128** Images; **130** Images; **131** Hillel Burger/Peabody Museum, Cambridge, MA; **132tl** Margaret Kawharu/BM; **132mr** Popperfoto; **132bl** BM; **132br** BM; **133** Collection of the Museum of New Zealand Te Papa Tongarewa, B.18702; **134** e.t. archive; **135** Tim Graham; **136** Michael O'Hanlon, Oxford; **137** Rogan Coles/ Redferns Music Library